Not Another Book About Italy

For Geoffrey

Not Another Book About Italy

Ann Rickard

NEW
HOLLAND

One

There really isn't a need for another book about Italy. We all know that. Look on the shelves in any travel section of any bookstore and you'll see more than enough books written about Italy. Beautiful books by erudite people who've bought old, uninhabitable Tuscan/Umbrian/Ligurian farmhouses and restored them into comfortable dwellings of infinite charm. These clever people seem to undertake this restoration with a minimum of fuss, all the while forming lifelong friendships with tight-knit locals and discovering a host of hidden talents including olive tree pruning and fresh pear preserving.

I'd love to write such a book a lovely tome filled with pages of evocative prose about fields of dancing sunflowers and groves of shimmering olive trees. I'd love to tell you about the simple joy of erecting a table under a giant fig tree after a rewarding day spent sanding old ceiling beams and discovering beautiful frescoes beneath years of mould on thick dining room walls. I'd introduce you to my new best friends from the village down the road, who join me at my table where we chargrill locally made sausages skewered with sprigs of rosemary (from my lovingly tended herb garden) over an open fire while drinking my self-bottled wine. At the end of our meal, we would reach up to pluck a perfectly ripe fig to serve with a chunk of gorgonzola and then talk on and on into the warm Tuscan night. And I'd have every paragraph punctuated with charming *italicised* Italian words and names.

'... At the *panetteria* in the *piazza* we pause during our *passeggiata* to greet Luigi and Mariuccia and, after many enthusiastic *ciao*s (for we now know them well enough to use the more intimate form of greeting rather than the formal *buon giorno*), we buy some freshly baked *panini* to eat with the *porchetta* slowly roasting at home in the old wooden oven we resurrected from its grave beneath the olive nets in the storage shed at the bottom of our property ...'

That really is how I'd like to write. But I have not lived in Tuscany/Umbria/Liguria for any length of time, let alone restored an old house or bonded with the local signoras or bottled pears.

As you will have noticed—being discerning readers (you must be, you bought this book)—you really do have to go and live in Italy and restore an old farmhouse before you can write dreamy prose with sexy Italian words in italics. There is absolutely no getting away with making things up; even an amateur would instantly pick up my mistakes ... I believe you do not take a *passeggiata* in the morning, which is when you would in fact be buying *panini* and saying *buon giorno*. A *passeggiata* is an evening stroll, the time when Italians don their good gear and go out into the streets to lick *gelati*, walk up and down, be seen and admired, stop to talk with friends and, in the case of the younger generation, flirt big-time.

So, having brought the italic thing to your attention right up front—and I am happy to say that you will be treated to many more *italicised* words throughout this book—let me say that I do have something to write about Italy and all its charms, frustrations and complexities. Probably nothing new, but maybe in a different way, a way that might connect with you and take you on a little Italian holiday, detouring just for a short while across the northern border into Switzerland.

But first, because I am a woman of a certain age, a small indulgence if you don't mind. Let me take a shuffle down memory lane to 1966 when I first met Italy, a time when the miniskirt was the height of fashion and I was twenty years old and owned a pair of legs that went all the way from Melbourne to Cairns (or London to Glasgow, depending on where you are reading this).

Back then, Naples was the first Italian city I visited. Not the best place to greet Italy, but there was no choice; it was the first European port of call the Italian ship made on its way from Melbourne to Southampton.

Like many young Australian women of the time, I was on my way to London to do the working holiday thing. I am in fact an English person—I was born there and my parents immigrated to Australia when I was about ten, but I have always felt a strong connection with my country of birth—and I wanted to return to work and live in lovely London and explore exciting Europe. Ships were the favoured form of travel then (a flight from Australia to England cost about the same as a small house) and if it took six weeks to get there, all the better—a holiday en route to the working holiday was all part of the experience.

An old Australian television documentary entitled *On Being a Sheila* was recently re-aired and it revealed, among many enlightening snippets, that in 1965 (I know it's a year before I'm talking about, but let's not be pedantic) the average Aussie sheila was expected to be a virgin when she married at the perfect age of twenty-four, and that 'tens of thousands' of us sailed off on ships to go and work in London. Tens of thousands!

Our blokes would come to see us off and sit around on the decks before the ship set sail. They would drink from beer cans and mutter romantic farewells between swigs. 'Down the hatch', they'd fondly say. Or, more meaningfully, 'Don't do anything I wouldn't do'. And, even better, 'Watch out for those continental blokes'. And watch out for them we did. From the very moment the ship left the wharf.

An Italian ship full of suave and randy Italian officers gave us an exciting and comprehensive introduction to the ways of Italians. Admittedly, it was only the ways of gold-braided, white-uniformed, worldly Italian men; men who had nothing on their minds except bedding every one of those tens of thousands of Australian girls. But, in 1966 to most Australian girls who had never been in the company of elegant men, they were thrilling ways. Sex was the only thing that mattered much to these men, followed—temporarily— by good food and the occasional hearty singalong ... and then it was time for sex again.

Even sailing the ship didn't appear particularly important, for the captain was the leader of the pack when it came to chasing the girls. Fortunately for me, during that particular trip in 1966 there were not the usual 'tens of thousands' of us on board. Just a couple of dozen. Most pleasing odds.

To be on the high seas on a ship full of continental blokes with roiling hormones and wives safely tucked at home was indeed a heady thing. We quickly learnt that to Italian men, having a wife did not mean the absence of a love life with the rest of the world's female population, should that be achievable. A wife was a nice thing to have, and well respected she was too, but why would she want to stand in the way of a full and satisfying sex life that did not include her?

This was my introduction to the Italian philosophy on love. Well, actually, I was introduced to the randy Italian half an hour before I even boarded the ship in Melbourne. The ship's doctor, standing importantly at the head of the queue in the quarantine section on the wharf, was checking everyone's inoculation booklets in a bored fashion. (Were we really required to have smallpox injections before entering the UK in 1966?) The doctor looked at my book, looked me up and down, lost his bored expression and told me to report to his surgery the next morning after the ship set sail.

I worriedly made my way to his surgery the next day clutching my inoculation booklet, certain I had contracted smallpox during the drive from my home in Melbourne's western suburbs to the wharf in Port Melbourne. When I sat in his office and nervously showed him my booklet again he leaned forward, brushed the book aside and whispered, 'Do you like to dance?'

Like to dance? Just what dancing had to do with smallpox inoculations I was to find out later in his cabin, but don't worry, I won't give you any unwanted detail—other than to say that between the doctor and the captain, I did a lot of dancing.

Until Naples, that is. Here the dancing abruptly halted as the wives boarded and stayed for the rest of the trip around to Southampton. These suave Italian men changed from *bons vivants* to submissive weaklings overnight. The captain's wife in particular was a stern-faced, bleak woman (no wonder, with a horny husband on the loose for most of the year) who stood on the upper decks outside his cabin and glared down onto the second-class decks at us butter-wouldn't-melt-in-our-mouths young girls who were crushed at the thought of going the rest of the trip to Southampton—a whole three days—without another dance.

But back to Naples. Dizzy with the awesome power I had over Italian men at that point, I could see only beauty in the often-maligned city. Where others saw slums I saw flower shops, where there were squalor and street kids I saw sunshine and sparkling sea scenes, where there was uncollected rubbish I saw only geraniums spilling from terracotta pots. And everywhere, men, men and more men.

Cries of *'Bella ragazza! Bella ragazza!'* followed me down every narrow cobblestoned street and were bellowed from every coffee shop and open window of passing cars. I had no idea what it meant but assumed it was something lusty and flattering, as it was always accompanied by a loud smacking of fingers to lips, lewd smiles and hearty whoops of appreciation.

It wasn't until 2000—after a lifetime of marriage, of ten happy years living in London and Southampton, of another twenty contented years bringing up a family in the outer suburbs of Melbourne, when I was about to embark on a holiday to Italy—that I bothered to seek out the words in my Italian dictionary. *Bella ragazza*, beautiful girl. Beautiful girl. How positively wonderful.

So there I was in 2000, about to go back to Italy for the first time in thirty years, excited and hopeful. But my 2000 look was very different to my 1966 look and, while the legs were obviously still as long, they now housed clusters of spidery veins and pockets of dimply cellulite. They hadn't attracted a smidge of flattery in decades.

I went off with no hope of eliciting a single *bella ragazza*, of course, but I did have a (deeply suppressed) expectation of at least one *bella donna*—beautiful woman—and maybe a little smacking of the fingers to lips, perhaps from one of the more discerning older Italian men. At the very least I could surely expect an appreciative glance from one of those leathery old blokes who sit about in *piazza*s all over Italy.

But, nothing. Italian men, now accustomed to an endless procession of beautiful women from all over the world streaming gorgeously through their streets and lying toplessly on their beaches and wearing almost nothing in their cafés, can't seem to summon up the enthusiasm for a *bella* anything any more.

But enough talk of men and sex and my conceit.

Why should I write a book about Italy, you could well ask, when so many others before me have already done so, and done so well? Because I can, I suppose. I am a writer. I earn my living by it. As a full-time feature writer for the *Sunshine Coast Daily* in Queensland, I write a lot. Every day. Thousands of words. I write even when I am on holiday; I just have to.

A few years ago I suddenly found that I had raised a son and two daughters and sent them off to earn their own livings and, when I'd overcome the surprise of having brought up three well-adjusted and delightful people, I realised I could go back to Italy. Often.

I took my laptop with me and kept a diary. At the end of each day in Rome, Portofino, Siena, Lucca, Sorrento, Capri, Santa Margherita and Positano, I wrote and wrote. I put down my observations in extensive detail then turned them into travel columns and sent them back to my newspaper in Australia, where they were published in my absence. On my return I was overwhelmed by the interest and feedback from my readers.

'We loved your stories about Italy; please write more about Italy', they said. Everyone, it seemed, wanted to read more about Italy. I don't know why this surprised me—apart from my perpetual surprise that anyone would be interested in reading anything I write—because Italy is, after all, fascinating to just about everyone.

Is it the Italians' unashamed love of life that attracts us so much? Will we ever understand how they manage to get the balance of work, fun, family and food so utterly right? The Italians embrace life like no other society in the world and I suspect they don't even know the secret themselves. It just happens.

Apart from the people and their exuberance, there is the thrill of the Italian landscape. It has everything from shadowed hills, vast lakes, dense forests, imposing mountains and one of the most spectacular coastlines in the world. And what about those Umbrian fields of sunflowers? And the rows of tall Tuscan cypress trees? The endless olive groves, the green vineyards, the rolling country hills?

All these clichés must be mentioned in any book about Italy and explored by every traveller. And I haven't even started talking about the museums yet, nor taken you inside one of the awesome high-ceilinged churches. The architecture, the history, the icons, the shopping, the restaurants, the cafés, the bars … it is little wonder we love to read about all things Italian.

To begin this book, I turned to the past, as you have seen. After my first visit to Italy in 1966 as a young single woman, I returned four years later as a young married woman. On the back of a big motorbike with my new husband (a Kiwi-turned-Aussie, not an Italian, damn it) I zoomed all over Italy for three sunny months.

We lived blissfully, joyously, on almost nothing. We packed all our possessions including the kitchen sink (a plastic washing-up tub, actually) on the motorbike, stayed in camp sites and slept in a tiny tent. We whooshed past lines of traffic to find small parking spots that no car could fit into right in the heart of Rome, Florence or Milan. We sat for hours on the ledge of the Trevi Fountain with almost no-one around us, arms around each other's shoulders; we threw in coins and drank Chianti poured into the little multi-coloured metallic picnic cups we took everywhere with us.

They really were heady, halcyon days. (Trying to do that, to capture the same romance thirty years later, with thousands of tourists clamouring and pushing around every monument, ended in acute frustration and a mutual promise to never try to relive the past again.)

In those days, on that trip, I also kept a diary, a small notebook I wrote in at the end each day.

'Do you think you could find that notebook?' I asked my Geoffrey all those years later as I sat staring into space, searching for inspiration to start this book. (Geoffrey keeps everything, including a bundle of love letters we wrote to each other in those passionate days and would probably make us both puke now should we ever be so stupid as to look at them.)

'Yes, I'm sure I could find it', he said and disappeared into the garage. Within half an hour he presented it to me. It was musty and smelly as hell, full of loose yellow pages of untidy handwriting. I opened it with excitement and expectation, looking forward to reading all the colourful detail I knew I had recorded of romantic gondola trips down the Grand Canal, culturally enlightening visits to museums, lazy days on hot Adriatic beaches and long warm nights by the lakes in northern Italy.

What a horrible shock. Where I expected to find detailed text, I found non-descriptive, pathetically short sentences.

Slept till 10 a.m. Left the camp at 11 a.m. Drove to a small place along the coast. Arrived around 2 p.m. Had a swim. Drove to the village. Friendly people.

Where the hell were we? I realise I was young, but surely I had enough sense to write down place names, observations, impressions … anything that might later bring memories back in some detail? I turned to another page.

Spent the day on the beach. It was nice. Went for a stroll.

Which beach? Where? What did we see? Who did we meet? What did we learn? How was the weather? I wanted to weep at the waste. Another page, and the most stupendous of all the inadequate entries.

Went to Florence. Saw David in the gallery. Most impressed. Drove out of Florence on hilly roads. Drove through Pisa. Took some photos. Found a camp. Shaved my legs.

Saw David and was 'most impressed'? *Shaved my legs?*

Yet I well remember walking straight up to David in the *Galleria dell'Accademia* (there was no roped-off area then). I clearly recall standing right beneath him, looking up at his enormous feet, his detailed toes and, looking way, way up past his huge muscled calves and bulging thighs, his fabulous willie.

I also remember not having to queue, not even for a minute. To think of the ease of getting up so close to all that awesome art in those days—and all I bothered to write was 'most impressed'. All the magnificent countryside outside Florence was recorded as 'hilly roads'. And as for poor old Pisa, all it got was: 'Drove through … Took some photos'.

I very nearly did shed a tear then. I threw the 'diary' in the bin, whereupon Geoffrey retrieved it and returned it to the mildewy box in the garage along with the fusty old love letters we will never (ever) read but must keep because Geoffrey is a cute sentimental old fool sometimes and cannot bear to throw anything out.

Now, if I have managed to keep your interest thus far with my rambling reminiscences, let me assure you it gets better. Now that I am no longer a silly young girl rushing around Italy seeking attention from married men, or gazing upon wondrous icons and dismissing them with capricious critiques, I really do have some interesting and fun observations about Italy and Italians.

And I intend to write them all in full—and quite possibly flamboyant—detail. But before we step into the next chapter, let me ask your indulgence, because I am a food writer as well as a feature writer and I sometimes tend to rant on a bit about some of the meals we consumed on this trip. But, as Italian cuisine is among the best in the world, I trust you will enjoy reading about it. (If you really cannot abide my flowery food prose, feel free to just skip those bits.) And forgive me, too, if Geoffrey and I zigzag around Italy in a gloriously unscheduled way, because this is really how we travelled—flitting from one place to another, sometimes backtracking and wandering around in circles. Add to that my penchant for ambling down memory lane with little stories about life in Australia and England, and you might occasionally wonder what on earth I am up to. But don't worry, I'll do my best not to confuse you … and I absolutely promise not to bore you.

Two

So, here we are, ready to take off to Italy for the summer, an ordinary middle-aged couple to join the hordes of ordinary middle-aged couples all over Europe. No doubt we will blend in all too easily with everyone else, although we refuse to wear those ridiculous bumbags around our thick waists and I long ago banned bermuda shorts and knee-high socks from Geoffrey's wardrobe. He in turn has forbidden me to wear a plastic sun visor or anything in the menopausal lavender colour favoured by many women my age.

We have fretted and fussed over our packing, not used to being away for such a long period, intimidated by our lack of travel-packing experience during the past thirty years. Should we take only light clothes? What if it gets cold at night? A cardie (daggy), a cashmere shawl (don't own one) or a pashmina (*so* yesterday)? Hair dryer or hot rollers? Walking shoes, sandals, dancing shoes? Jeans, tailored slacks, skirts? In the end we pack the lot, including a large stock of every kind of toiletry imaginable, just in case I run out in the middle of Tuscany. Four jars of moisturiser, two of cleansing cream, a giant tube of foot scrub and a tub of organic foot mask. Why my feet should suddenly require a facial (or should that be footial?) in the Tuscan fields I am not quite sure, especially as they've never been fortunate enough to have one in their long life at home, but the urge to take girly pampering products to Italy is so strong it overcomes me.

This urge is, of course, deeply regretted at the airport check-in counter, where our overweight bags annoy a pedantic staff member, who makes us unpack them and move anything heavy into our hand luggage. Rifling through an over-packed suitcase on the floor in front of a large crowd of impatient people who can see your full-scale bra-with-enough-wire-to-reinforce-the-Sydney-Harbour-Bridge is one of life's more humiliating experiences and should be a lesson to all you over-packers. Trust me, travelling light, even if it means wearing the same T-shirt and shorts for weeks and washing out your knickers in the sink every night, is preferable to publicly rummaging through your suitcase at a busy airport.

Our first stop in Italy is actually Zürich, which you astute readers would know happens to be in Switzerland. I apologise for the detour, but we are first visiting our Swiss friends Charlie and Eva, who live near us in Noosa for the Australian spring and summer and spend the European summer in their hometown of Locarno, on the Swiss–Italian border. Charlie and Eva are retired but fit and slim and attractive and sprightly, and they insisted we visit them first in Locarno before we did Italy. The fact that they happen to rent a summer apartment in Santa Margherita on the Italian Riviera every year and have invited us to use it at our whim adds to their general fabulousness.

We love having friends like Charlie and Eva. (These are not their real names, by the way, I changed them after reading Peter Mayle's splendid *Toujours Provence*, in which he said that after his first book, *A Year in Provence*, was published, people kept turning up in his driveway and leaping out at him from the bushes in his front garden. I wouldn't want people flocking to Locarno in search of Charlie and Eva. Not that *you* would do such a thing, of course.) We love the way they live, and we are about to love the way we live when we are with them. Charlie and Eva are darlings; generous, sensitive and intelligent people who both speak Italian, English, German and Spanish. Their Locarno home is a long single-storey stone house perched high on a terraced hill dotted with other charming houses. Their house is flanked by a deep gorge and overlooks the vast splendour of Lake Maggiore to the snowcapped mountains beyond. From their balcony they can see across the lake to Italy. Their garden is surrounded by stone walls with Roman fountains and is a profusion of tall hollyhocks, red roses, giant azaleas, pink rhododendrons, yellow tulips and stately yuccas. Among the mass of colour, fish ponds brim with life and small nooks and leafy dells house little tables perfect for sitting at while lingering over a morning coffee or sipping an evening glass of wine and peering out through the foliage to the breathtaking lake views.

It's all picture-postcard perfect and we feel as though we've stepped into a travel magazine. And when we wake the next morning to the chime of distant church bells, we're suspicious. Surely this is an impossible dream? Some cruel god is going to look down at us any minute, chuckle spitefully, snap his fingers and tell us to bugger off back home to reality and routine.

It's June and sunny and warm. Charlie and Eva invite friends around for dinner to entertain us, although we really need nothing more than to laze around and lap up all this beauty. Eva insists on cooking alone all afternoon and sends us off with Charlie to explore the outrageously pretty town of Brione, just a kilometre from their home.

Everywhere we look we see charm. Bright flowers spill from window boxes and hanging baskets in every cobbled street, shops and cafés look as though they belong in children's books, and the omnipresent backdrop of the magnificent mountains thrills us. This is a wonderful introduction to Europe after a break of thirty years. Brione is the kind of place you look at in travel brochures and picture yourself standing right there in one of its cobbled streets beneath a hanging basket of magnificent colour. You can clearly see yourself sitting at a pavement café sipping coffee beneath a cheery umbrella thinking happy thoughts. It's the kind of place that makes you wish you were European.

Back home, Eva has made her special ravioli—neat little pasta squares filled with sage and then sautéed in butter. She snips rocket from her window box and tosses it into a large wooden bowl with cress and other mysterious leaves from her garden. Thin slices of veal are waiting to be fried in olive oil and served with small roasted potatoes and beans cooked with onion and olive oil until meltingly soft. Charlie and Eva's friends arrive: Tony and Hannah from the local International Club and the chic French neighbour from the small house down the hill who wishes to be addressed only as Madame. She looks fifty; we learn later she is almost eighty. Eighty years of French elegance and perfect preservation.

Loud, joyous greetings are made followed by light kisses, starting with the left cheek, then right, then left again. We take to this European three-kiss greeting with enthusiasm but it is to confuse us for the rest of our stay. Just when we think we've got it right, they switch back to two kisses, one per cheek, and we are left mid-kiss, or worse, planting a clumsy one on the tip of a retreating nose or ear and sometimes, to our horror, smack bang on lips if the kissee's head hasn't swivelled quickly enough. No tongues, though.

After the introductions, everyone in the group switches to English for our benefit, which makes us feel like awkward oafs. Tony is a retired airline executive; he and Hannah lived for years in London and New York. Madame is far too overwhelming and aloof to be questioned about her background. We sense it will be revealed in tiny scraps, if and when she is ready—this turns out to be never, during our brief acquaintance. Everything about her screams out European style and easy elegance. She is quite awesome and the others are respectful to her; we are terrified.

We sit in the grotto section of the house, a stone-walled cave-like dining room that still feels open thanks to big folding doors that swing right back to let the glorious garden meander inside. Low-hanging chandeliers are switched on, candles are lit in dark corners, a Bordeaux is fetched from Charlie's wine cellar and Eva brings in her ravioli and tiny bowls of buttery sauce to sit on small warming burners. Glasses are clinked jovially as the conversation turns to Swiss politics, and we listen attentively. Everyone in Switzerland, it seems, is fed up with the government's lackadaisical approach to keeping out the flood of refugees from Italy (via Croatia) and just about every other suffering country in the world, according to the Swiss. Charlie has plenty to say on the matter and the noise level rises, which could also have something to do with his frequent trips to the cellar and the continual happy clinking of glasses. The table is thumped vigorously to emphasise a point and hands are waved frantically in the air; Eva tries to settle everyone down with soothing offers of more food, and it is difficult to get a word in. The evening is one of the most stimulating we can remember. Some time between the tender veal and a generous slice of Eva's chocolate pear gâteau I dare to wonder if that unkind god is watching and has decided we've had way too much of a good thing.

We have, like everyone, heard stories about the Swiss being pedantic and finicky, stiff and formal, but these people are as relaxed and easygoing (and loud) as any Australian. They treat us with friendly charm and welcome us into their lives as though we have long been close friends.

Our only previous experience of the Swiss came in the form of a frighteningly intelligent sixteen-year-old exchange student who stayed with us for six months. It took her a little time to relax with us, and I well remember making a mental note to be very careful what I asked her to do after she told us of her outrage at a former Australian host mother who once required her to waitress for a dinner party—to serve at the table and, worse, to don an apron. 'I do not do this, I am not a waitress', our Swiss student angrily told me. She knew her role in society and it did not include waiting on tables.

She took about a month to warm to us and when she finally did, it was only because of her lost panties. Allow me to explain. She continually lost them and this naturally caused me alarm because as her host mother I was expected to watch out for the upkeep of her morals. But when she told me she was losing them in the house (her underwear, not her morals), I relaxed. I am always losing my own—in the washing machine, in that flint-catcher-thing in the dryer, in the laundry … innocent places. We searched everywhere in the house for her missing panties and they finally turned up in Geoffrey's underwear drawer. She was a believer in the plain style of knickers, navy blue or black Bonds that were easily mistaken for men's, and Geoffrey had been obliviously wearing her panties for weeks. After we had stopped laughing and she had disinfected all her underwear, she settled right in and became one of us. We had bonded over her Bonds, so to speak.

Every morning we eat crusty bread, homemade cherry jam, sweet nectarines and strong coffee in one of the garden's leafy dells, protected from the morning sunshine. Charlie tells us we are lucky; we know it. But he's actually referring to the weather.

'It is not always so sunny in Locarno', he says. 'Sometimes it rains this time of year.'

We spend lazy days in the garden recuperating and recharging for another of Charlie's forays up into the mountains. He drives us over the Gotthard Pass, a spectacular and winding journey over the snowcapped Alps. Charlie skilfully drives around the hairpin bends, the road climbing so high that its side is stacked with tall, solid snow banks, the snow not yet melted by the summer sun. We make wonderful journeys through fairytale villages—Interlaken, Lugano and Bellinzona, to Grindelwald, where we eat giant ice-cream sundaes in a lively café beneath the majestic Eiger and Jungfrau mountains.

In St Moritz we lunch on salads and pasta in the dining room of an old and quiet hotel. Later we wander the neat streets to peer into the windows of expensive shops and imagine what this glamorous place must be like at the height of the winter ski season, with the rich lovelies packing the town.

Charlie takes us out on twelve-hour days, driving us over high and jagged mountains and through unimaginably beautiful countryside with deep ravines, terrifying passes and green slopes. We open the car windows to inhale the Swiss country air and look high up to see tiny stone farmhouses perched on top of forbidding mountains.

'One single farmer will take his cows up there for the summer months', Charlie tells us. 'The grass is very sweet up there and full of wild flowers; the cows love it.' Indeed, the fat brown cows, all wearing cowbells, look very content, well fed, gloating almost. 'They will feast like kings and produce the creamiest milk, which the farmer will make into cheese, all done inside those stone farm-houses', Charlie says. 'The cheese is much in demand by locals.'

At the end of each day, we feel we have landscape lag, beauty overload and vista overkill. We need to lie down and close our eyes and peer at the images in our head for a while. Which we do, in readiness for more fabulousness the next day.

Later, as I hunch over my laptop writing this, I look back to my 1970 journal with little hope of tracing the days back then of our journey on the motorbike over the Swiss Alps. But I am curious to see if I had recorded anything, for I remember sitting for hours on the back of the bike driving over spectacular scenes. Of course, the diary revealed nothing: *Drove all day; took ages to find a camp.*

Angry all over again at my stupidity, I go to the old photo albums. They smell even mustier than the diary, the little square photos faded beneath sweaty plastic layers. But there I am in Switzerland, standing next to the motorbike by the side of an anonymous road in front of a glorious backdrop of mountains. I am wearing a tatty blue sweater and black pants as well the brightest of blue eye shadow, with thick black eyeliner drawn above and below my eyes. I have a haircut so short it's a wonder my ears didn't freeze over and drop off. I am holding a large snowball. On the back of the photo my scrawl enlightens: *Switzerland, 1970. Me holding a snowball.*

We have spent memorable days in Switzerland. Charlie and Eva are the sort of hosts everyone aspires to be. They have managed to present extravagant meals without any fuss after long days of driving over mountains. Food has appeared as if by magic, dishes seem to have slipped into the dishwasher by themselves and the garbage has obligingly taken itself outside and graciously disappeared without bothering any of us.

But now it is time to go to Italy, and Charlie and Eva are coming with us for the first part. Charlie, a master planner who leaves nothing to chance—even playing rousing marching music at eight every morning to ensure we get out of bed with suitable enthusiasm for another busy day—gets out his maps, brochures and notebooks. He tunes into the radio for weather forecasts while

Eva puts on the coffee and lays the table with her cherry jam and bread rolls once again.

We are going to Rigoli, just outside Pisa, to spend a night at Villa di Corliano. The hotel brochure tells us that the villa has its 'prestigious seat in the sixteenth century' and is 'presently the residence of Agostini Veronesi della Seta Counts, Strido Counts, one of the most famous families of the Italian nobility'. We're impressed. The present Count still lives on-site. The brochure also mentions that the villa has a 'suggestive breakfast room', and we look forward to it; a bit of suggestion at breakfast doesn't seem like a bad way to start the day.

Brochures translated into English in foreign countries always amuse me. I remember once in the Greek Islands—it was Paros, I think—reading a brochure that extolled the delights of a hotel with underground caves and tunnels. 'Deep in the intestines of the hotel,' it told us, 'you will find many exciting discoveries.' Unfortunately we never got around to exploring the hotel's intestines on that occasion, but we did laugh a lot.

So we take our leave of Charlie and Eva's fabulous home, sighing with sadness as we drive off, feeling that something important has happened to us in Locarno but we are not quite sure what. Have we developed a better appreciation for the majesty of nature? Did we experience a cultural experience of significant importance? Do we now have a deeper bond with our friends? Or are we melancholy simply to be leaving behind the pleasure of Charlie and Eva's toilet? Perhaps only in Switzerland would you find a toilet with a built-in bottom-washer. A blissful invention. With just a small press of a discreet button on the side of the toilet, up comes a gentle swish of deliciously warm water, perfectly aimed with just the right amount of pressure. Could there be a nicer way to kick off a day in a pretty Swiss town? But let's not get into this now. Not after all this talk of magnificent mountains and breathtaking gorges and beautiful Swiss vistas. We'll save toilet talk for later.

Charlie is confident on the Italian roads. He races along the autostrada at terrifying speeds, changes lanes like a racing-car driver and approaches the tollbooths with self-assurance, calling out like a seasoned Italian (which he could almost qualify as, living as close to them as he does) to toll collectors, waving his money at them on his rush through. We turn off the autostrada into the Tuscan countryside and discover all the beautiful clichés right before us, all the beauty we have read about in books—the rolled haystacks, the neat fields, the quaint stone houses. The hilly roads force Charlie to slow down and we sit back and drink it all in. We're lulled by the peace, the sensuous countryside, the Tuscan dream. Then, on a straight road near Rigoli, surrounded by silver-green olive trees and fields of swaying sunflowers, we see something not mentioned in any of our travel books. Prostitutes. Black ones.

There are a dozen of them on this particular road, each with her allocation of Tuscan country space. Each wears a different version of the prostitute's uniform: tight hotpants, cropped tops, micro miniskirts, long trashy boots and sky-high stilettos. Some have set up comfortable little camps by the side of the road; a folding chair for the wait and a beach umbrella for protection from the hot sun. They sit and swing shapely black legs in invitation, their lovely round faces seeking out potential clients as cars pass. They peer into our car, their expectant white smiles in glossy black faces quickly turning to indifference as we—obviously four non-clients—stare at them with rude curiosity. We are mystified by this conundrum. Black hookers in the middle of the Tuscan countryside? The situation has us agog. Where have they come from? And, apart from the obvious, what on earth are they doing here? We are so curious we miss our turn and are forced to go back down the same road. It's a good excuse for another look. Dozens of questions ricochet inside the car. Who are they? Why are they here in the country and not in the city? What little business must they get here in the country? We have no answers; we don't even have a theory.

We notice that one of the ladies has negotiated successfully with a parked motorist, so we stop our car a discreet distance and watch. She leads him a little way into the sunflower fields and we stare, fascinated and giggling, as the sunflowers dance energetically.

Charlie and Eva tell us we are unlikely to find out why the prostitutes are plying their trade in this idyllic country scene, as it would be impolite to ask in the next village. And we certainly could not offend the Count at Villa di Corliano just a dozen kilometres away by asking such an indecorous question, so we are left to wonder as we continue on our way.

But we do find out. Weeks later as we sit on our sun-drenched balcony in our Santa Margherita villa and read the international newspapers, we spot a small article that explains it all. Women from Nigeria have been lured to Italy on the promise of jobs and prosperity, only to find on arrival that neither exists. They are forced into prostitution to repay their 'benefactors', who have charged them an exorbitant ninety million lire—about ten thousand Australian dollars—to leave poverty behind in Africa for the same thing thousands of miles away in Italy.

The newspaper warns tourists to watch out for more than the usual icons they expect to see in Italy that summer. African prostitutes will be on duty outside the Vatican, loitering on the Spanish Steps, hanging around the Leaning Tower of Pisa and working the queues outside the Uffizi Gallery, it tells us. An unusual sight among the expected symbols of Italy, you must agree, and one of the more contradictory but powerful images we will always have of Tuscany.

Three

The first thing we do in the afternoon at Villa di Corliano is discover the 'suggestive breakfast room'. We find it down a steep staircase and through a succession of heavy doors and passageways. It holds no hint of suggestion but is dotted with small tables with blue tablecloths set for the morning fare. We look forward to strong espresso and suggestion in the morning but, for now, we must explore the rest of the villa.

Villa di Corliano is between Pisa and Lucca, in Rigoli, a small, quiet village with wonderful weathered old men and wrinkled brown old women sitting in the doorways of rustic stone houses that edge right onto the roadside. Owned by the noble Agostini family, the villa now operates as a luxury hotel and is obviously a landmark and major attraction of the area.

The villa is an imposing square stone building with a long circular gravel driveway leading to the steps at the large front doors.

The garden is host to a giant old tree with a trunk wider than a few people, its branches forming an enormous green umbrella over long tables. In the background are those lovely green Tuscan hills.

A grand bed dominates our room on the second level. The iron bedhead is inlaid with an oval of padded gorgeousness—beautiful hand-embroidered roses that one of Count Agostini's ancestors toiled over perhaps? I choose to think so, as I want to savour all the romance going in this place. In the wide hallway outside our room marble-topped tables hold imposing sculptures of hand-some heads. Count Agostini's ancestors again? It is quite heady for a short while to think that we can actually live here surrounded by such richness. We shower and change and descend the white marbled staircase to meet Charlie and Eva with happy hearts. Sitting in the main salon, our jaws drop at the scale of grandeur. We order *spumante*, the sweet fizz the Italians love to drink before dinner, a drink we Australians gave up a few decades ago and wish never to revisit. But there is no choice here if we want to drink bubbles, and we do, because this place calls for a cork to be popped.

We gape around us. The high frescoed ceilings are covered with angels and cherubic-looking little boys peering out from elaborate chariots pulled by graceful horses. A huge chandelier twinkles in crystal glory in the centre of the ceiling. A marble statue, Madonna—or at least a plaintive woman in flowing marble robes—looks at us from a corner. We sink down into couches of golden velvet and sip the sweet fizz. Charlie, a super-clever man who has memory of just about every word he has ever read (and there have been billions of them during a lifetime of study and law practice), gives us the history of this place, which I have now forgotten because I am not a super-clever woman and do not have memory of every word I have seen or heard. This is just as well for you, lovely readers, as I'm sure a lot of historical detail would bore the pants off you and we really do need to get on with the story.

It is enough to say that this is a mighty impressive old villa. And for the moment we have this grand salon all to ourselves. We congratulate each other on our good fortune to be able to stay, if only for one night, in a place of such utter refinement. As we sit and sip we realise there are guestrooms leading off this awesome salon. A handsome couple comes in with smart suitcases and expensive-looking hand luggage, then disappears through a frescoed door into one of the rooms. But then a scruffy T-shirted family of at least five piles untidily into the gorgeous salon with bulging backpacks, big walking boots *and a mongrel dog*. Although they look absolutely out of place in this setting, they appear perfectly at ease and confident of the welcome they will receive. They too disappear through a frescoed door, only to immediately and loudly come back out again. Several raucous trips are made to their car for more backpacks and ugly junk, with the dog yelping and jumping all over them and sniffing the wonderful furniture before readying its leg to lift against the frescoes. Only a loud exclamation from me draws the family's attention to the dog and they stop it from peeing up the lovely wall. We are horrified, but then embarrassed by our snooty assumption that this place should be reserved for people such as ourselves. Obviously the Count couldn't care less who stays in his historical villa as long as they pay the bill and enable him to continue living in the style of his forebears.

And where is this Count, anyway? I want to meet him.

We wander in the gardens with our *spumante* and take photos of each other standing beneath the giant tree, stretching our arms out as wide as possible to later show (bore?) our friends back home with gloating stories of this beautiful place. It is still daylight and very bright, but definitely time for dinner at nine o'clock, so into the Count's dining room we troop, praying that the scruffy family and its dog have decided to eat in the village down the road. Fortunately they have. *Snobs.*

The dining room, unlike the salon, is not grand. Plain white-washed walls have been left bare but for a couple of ordinary prints. It is the wine racks holding hundreds of beautiful and old wines with intriguing labels lining the walls that do all the talking here. Nothing more is needed to create an atmosphere of wealth and nobility. We relax and choose a bottle.

'*Brunello di Montalcino*, it must be, it must', Charlie says authoritatively. 'Only one of Tuscany's most famous and desired wines will do in this fine place.' We are more than happy to let Charlie choose the wine and we settle down to *composizione di antipasti di mare* (seafood antipasto) and *risotto ai fiori di zucca e tartufi neri di Norcia* (risotto with pumpkin flowers and black truffles from Norcia).

The dining room is empty but for us and a well-fed German couple. She fascinates me; she is quite overweight and has terrible home-dyed blonde hair. She bends her head to her plate and does not look up nor speak during the entire evening. She concentrates on getting through course after course, her jaws chomping up and down, up and down. He spends most of the night either watching her, smoking or staring into space. Soup, risotto, spaghetti, steak, salad, potatoes, vegetables, dessert, cheese; it all goes in. Brassy blonde head down, she eats with a thoroughness that keeps me staring rudely. The next morning she is at it again. Not in the least interested in the suggestive ambience of the breakfast room, she fills her plate with a mini-mountain of salami, ham and cold sausage from the buffet table before heading back for cheeses, bread rolls and jams. I love being near people like this because they make me feel better about my own lack of willpower at the table.

As we are checking out, a man wearing a beautifully cut blazer and grey pants is elegantly hanging around the small reception area. This, surely, is the elusive Count Agostini? The receptionist's answer to my whispered question assures us it is. He is talking to the scruffy guests with the dog, and this gives me courage to approach him myself. I am determined to speak to him, to take his photo.

I wait and wait for the scruffs to disappear then approach him, hand outstretched, big friendly smile on my face. My first, and most probably last, encounter with Italian nobility begins when he takes my hand, but unfortunately he has just put a toffee in his mouth (those ubiquitous charity sweets that sit, usually untouched, on reception counters all over the world) and has a chewy mass of toffee stuck between his teeth.

'*Caramella*', the receptionist explains, obviously embarrassed that a distinguished royal personage is unable to speak because a sweet is stuck to his teeth. I pretend it is the most normal thing in the world for me to introduce myself to an Italian Count who is sucking on a toffee, and do what I always do when I'm embarrassed: talk a great load of garbage, very quickly.

'Crap, crap, crap', I say brightly while he sucks and chews.

'Rubbish, garbage, balderdash', I continue rapidly, trying to look anywhere but at his mouth.

'Blah, blah, yadda, yadda, crap, crap, blah, blah', I persist, now lightly perspiring.

An age passes but the wretched *caramella* finally dissolves and the Count can now give me his full attention. Fortunately for me he does not speak English and has not understood a word of my blithering rubbish. (At this stage, my Italian extends only to *buon giorno* and *dov'è il bagno?*, and I doubt our awkward situation will be saved by me saying, 'good morning, where is the toilet?'.) However, the Count is courteous and every inch Italian charm, and agrees to pose with me in the gardens by one of his lovely fountains. While he jabbers happily in Italian, I crap on happily in English; the result is several impressive photos of me with Italian royalty in luxurious gardens and one day, when I get to know you better, you can come around to my house and look at my photo albums. (I really shouldn't admit to this, but because I am an honest person, I will … as we drive off with Charlie and Eva, they break the disappointing news: this wasn't the Count at all, but a mere manager. The hotel receptionist had misunderstood my question and assumed I had asked if the man was the manager, and Charlie and Eva, understanding every Italian word spoken, had been too nice to tell me while they snapped endless photos. But don't you tell anyone.)

We drive north through Piemonte with Charlie and Eva. We savour every minute, because in a few days they will leave us on our own to combat the terrifying roads and frightening Italian drivers. While with Charlie and Eva, we sit secure in the back seat of the car as they confidently lead us all over northern Italy. We happily allow them to speak sternly to bored tollbooth operators, read foreign maps, ask roadworkers for complicated directions and, best of all, understand the answers. They drive us on flat roads past signs with lovely, familiar names—Parma, Alba, Asti— and through rice fields where the arborio rice is grown for those delicious risottos.

Charlie, our guide, encyclopaedia, beloved driver and adored speaker of the Italian language, tells us that the Piemontese consider themselves the best cooks in Italy and that Piemonte is home to the most delicious food in the country. 'This land produces excellent wines and the good rice for the risotto', he says. 'So it is only natural that it is the home of some of the most outstanding cuisine in the world.' And we are on our way to try some.

Eva's brother belongs to an epicurean club in Switzerland and travels Europe with a bunch of like-minded friends in search of good food and wine. They seek out small *trattorias*, busy bistros, grand dining rooms and intimate cafés in Italy, France, Germany and Spain. They especially like to hear word-of-mouth recommendations and adore making exciting discoveries, some little-known place no tourist has discovered, an out-of-the-way restaurant only the locals know about. We are heading for one of these discoveries right now. Named Balin, it sounds decidedly un-Italian, but Eva's brother and his gourmet mates assure us it is something very special indeed.

We drive through uninteresting landscape and unappealing towns, certain that Eva's brother has given us a bum steer. The blue sky even clouds over as if to warn us away.

'This could be it', Eva says. 'My brother told me it is no more than a hole in the wall, a place you would never step inside because it looks so terrible.'

This place certainly fits the bill. Uncared-for red brick façades of what look like abandoned warehouses line the roads, but in the middle of the gloom is a small splash of whitewash. A building of great underwhelmingness with barred windows is made a little brighter by a small wooden pergola over the door from which hang two baskets filled with colourful petunias. A trail of ivy flourishes up one beam of the pergola, giving us small hope that we might find good things inside, for this is indeed Balin.

Eva is understandably nervous; this is her brother's suggestion and we have driven many miles to enjoy lunch here. But inside we find an oasis of rustic style and joyous welcome. Tables are set with white linen, silver cutlery and big tempting wine glasses. Intriguingly shaped bottles of local olive oils, multicoloured sacks of rice and bottles of local wine are displayed on benches, on shelves, on top of the fireplace, on wine barrels, on the floor, on every available space. The waiter sits us down with much flapping of starched serviettes and invites us to trust him, to wait and see, to enjoy whatever comes out of the kitchen. A lengthy discussion ensues, because Charlie has to drive for the rest of the afternoon and Eva has to navigate, so we do not want a multi-course extravaganza that will see us in dire need of a siesta.

Much is spoken of *primi piatti solo* (first courses only), but the waiter will have none of this. Descriptive gestures are made involving the sweeping of fingers away in a long upside-down arc from the top lip. We cannot imagine what he is recommending.

'An unknown sea creature with long whiskers', Charlie translates. 'He wants us to have it with a glass of *spumante*.' Not the *spumante* again. But yes, we are close to Asti and that's where *spumante* is made and, we are told, it is mandatory that we have it with the unknown long-whiskered sea creature. And it is indeed a perfect match and puts us in an anticipatory mood. We have no idea what the sea creature is but it looks and tastes like a yabbie. Maybe they are farming yabbies in the rice fields down the road—who knows?

The service is attentive and friendly, and the agreeable clanging noises coming from the kitchen suggest great things to come. The surroundings are so perfectly Italian that we don't care about anything other than being here and relishing everything about the experience. A bottle of local wine is opened and again there is much discussion, because Charlie likes his red wine a little chilled. Buckets of ice come out. The waiter is shocked. Charlie is pleased.

Delicious small treats keep coming: a meaty terrine, some grilled eggplant and zucchini, small slices of fish with tomato sauce, roasted goat (we think).

We are alone in the restaurant; it is a weekday and the whole area appears very quiet. But then a large family pours in and takes seats at a long table—the hubbub begins and we give ourselves over completely to the Italian experience.

We think we have finished eating; we have had about six courses and, although small, they have been rich and filling. But then, to our delight, out of the kitchen comes the waiter wheeling a trolley on which sits a huge parmesan wheel the size of a car tyre. It has been hollowed out and filled with steaming risotto. He guides it to our table and digs a huge spoon deep down into the well of creamy rice. He lunges and stirs—theatrically, we think, for our benefit, but no—to stir up little flakes of parmesan inside the hollow to add flavour to the risotto. The scene is so unexpected, so country Italian that we want to clap and cheer. Instead, we leap up to take half a dozen photos.

The table of Italians, obviously locals who do not linger over seven courses like us but go straight to their own risotto, are clearly amused by our enjoyment of what must be commonplace for them. By the end of the meal, the Italians are curious about us. Some of them speak English and have overheard our conversation. One wants to speak to Geoffrey and me but we are suddenly shy, feeling like gawky tourists, not confident talking to strangers. We rush outside and take photos of the unremarkable building exterior for

Eva's brother, then drive off, congratulating ourselves on walking into a memorable experience.

Charlie has planned one more day on the road before taking us to the summer apartment in Santa Margherita. We drive to Carrara, the mountain range in the middle of Tuscany where Michelangelo chose the huge blocks of marble for his sculptures. Very few Australians who visit Tuscany ever talk of Carrara. Maybe this is because the town itself is nothing remarkable, even though some of its streets are paved with marble. Most people are content to drive by because viewing the mountains from the distance is thrilling enough. What appear to be snowcapped peaks from afar turn out to be huge veins of marble close up.

We drive into the town first, then stop and buy fresh bread and ripe smelly cheese and eat it by the side of the road. Then we begin the drive up the steep mountains, passing dozens of nursery-style garden centres full of massive marble slabs the size of small cara-vans lying carelessly around the yards. There is marble everywhere, on the front of buildings, on balustrades, on statues, in steps. It's quite amazing.

Charlie relates an old legend of a clumsy angel who caused the birth of these mountains. Apparently the angel was flying over Italy and took a break over Carrara for a snooze. Another angel woke him and he jumped up and hit a big sack full of precious white mar-ble, which fell to the ground and formed the chain of mountains ... or something like that.

But of course that's a bit of nonsense. What is real is that Michelangelo spent some time in Carrara in the early sixteenth century choosing his marble, and it is exhilarating now for us to sit and stare at the mountains and try to picture him here. How he ever carved the marble out from the side of these mountains without technology, or how he got it down from those great heights without even the benefit of a four-wheel drive let alone a dirty big truck, is beyond imagination. We look up and wonder how many thousands of people died bringing the marble down; we could add the four of us to that number as huge trucks with massive loads of marble slabs thunder down the mountain past us as we drive up it. One careless moment and we will be squashed under tons of Carrara marble. It's thrilling, frightening and quite humbling.

We can only drive about three-quarters of the way up the mountain before warnings and fenced-off areas forbid us from going any further. It is like a city up here with teams of people, machinery, trucks and workmen's sheds sitting atop immense carved-out ledges of marble. We inch our way up as far as possible, stare for a long time at the surreal scene of white carved mountain before us, and then do what everyone on holiday does—head to the souvenir shop. There is always one, isn't there? No matter how high, remote, deep or far flung the attraction, you will always find somebody selling something, and why should Carrara be any different?

We wander into a shop crammed with crappy marble stuff made from all the little bits of marble rejects. Actually, it isn't all crappy, some of it is pretty good. We shun the mini statues of David, and the same goes for all the other miniature replicas of famous statues. But I can't resist the little marble olive bowls that I will rave on endlessly about back home every time I serve my guests a stuffed olive. I am also very smitten with the little wine corks with shiny round Carrara marble knobs on the end, and spend the equivalent of a hundred dollars on the little blighters to take home. They are for small gifts in the future whenever I am invited to someone's home for dinner—so much more impressive than the usual potted plant, you must agree, and a perfect excuse to forever bring up the subject of my fabulous trip to Carrara. Later, back in Australia when I had given out about twenty of these wine stoppers, I used one myself (and not just because I usually drink an entire bottle of wine in one go). I should have guessed it would be useless. It lasted all of two minutes before the marble ball on the end sadly departed from the cork bit.

I now have a kitchen drawer full of worthless Carrara marble balls, as do many of my friends. Actually, I have an entire household full of crappy stuff that doesn't work. I am unable to pass up anything that looks halfway interesting, especially on those compelling shopping channels on the telly. I once bought a battery-operated light that floated in the loo so that when you got up in the night you were guided to your toilet by an eerie green glowing light. I found this an irresistible buy at the time when a middle-aged man on television told me how this light had changed his life. He had gone from a loser fumbling around and stubbing his toes in a dark bedroom to a goal-oriented man of purpose and intent— all because he could walk confidently and directly to his toilet in the middle of the night. I loved that light even though it proved to be magnificently useless and worked for only a few days before it succumbed, I suppose, to death by being peed on.

Four

I am not a good passenger in the car in Italy. Oh, I'm fine in the backseat when Charlie, an experienced, multilingual, used-to-driving-on-the-right-hand-side-of-the-road European is at the wheel. But put me in the front seat alone when Geoffrey, an inexperienced, monolingual, used-to-driving-on-the-left-hand-side-of-the-road Australian is at the wheel and I turn into a quivering heap of uncertainty.

It is with this thought in mind that we spend the last few days with Charlie and Eva in Santa Margherita before we must collect our hire car and drive ourselves. They have brought us to their summer apartment and intend to leave and head back to Locarno so we can enjoy Italy by ourselves.

'Don't leave us alone', I beg them. It's a bit dramatic, I know, but I really don't want them to go. But as I have said, they are generous and sensitive people and think we want our own space. We don't. We love their company and the feisty, over-bottles-of-red-wine discussions on all matters, from politics to xenophobia to history to grandchildren. We love to have the responsibility for driving lie with someone experienced on the Italian roads. We have no inclination to take to the frantic roads ourselves with the blood-thirsty drivers and we certainly do not want to spend frustrating days searching for non-existent parking spaces. But we do wish to explore Italy a little further than Santa Margherita, so we must simply brace ourselves for *la macchina* (the car).

But in the meantime, what can I tell you about Santa Margherita? It is in the north and sits in the armpit of Italy (not a romantic description, but it should enable you to go straight to it on the map) on the Ligurian coast, part of the Italian Riviera. Its closest city is Genoa, a short train ride away. Travel books describe Santa Margherita as the 'pearl of the Ligurian coast' and we are not about to disagree. It nestles (they always nestle, don't they? Although sometimes they huddle, and occasionally they even snuggle) in a rocky shore and is surrounded by buildings in multi-hued shades of red, brown and yellow. It is a holiday town of infinite charm, a tourist paradise and one in which, it seems the day we arrive, every family from Europe and England has chosen to holiday. We fall hopelessly in love with it the minute we arrive.

I know travel writers are expected to avoid such clichéd towns; their job is to explore the difficult-to-get-to places, to bring you tales of dangerous mountain treks in Nepal and scary confrontations with tall African natives wearing dinner plates in their lips. Not for them a story about a steaming risotto in a parmesan wheel in Piemonte; more likely a rollicking yarn of sitting down to stir-fried black rat with garlic-and-ginger sauce in some remote province of China. These writers would no doubt sneer with disdain at me (and I certainly hope that's not what you are doing right now) but I happen to love Italian tourist towns for all the reasons others hate them. I especially love them for their comforts, colours and shoe shops, and we'll talk more about shoes later. As touristy as some of the Italian seaside towns are, they are not home to McDonald's or theme parks or ugly condominium buildings, and this saves them from being over-the-top clichés. I have waited and saved for many years to visit such places; I have spent a lifetime living in suburbia paying off mortgages, bringing up children, sitting through hours of their stupendously boring calisthenics concerts (only to wake up and clap enthusiastically when my own little princess came on) and driving pimply teenagers several million miles all over the country to basketball/netball/piano/karate practice, and it is time for indulgence.

Sorry about that. Having gotten that out of the way, let's go back to Santa Margherita.

Its streets are so very pretty, and right now they have their most flirty summer outfits on. The geraniums are rioting in hanging baskets, window boxes and garden beds all over town—and the riot police don't seem to be doing a damned thing about it. Jaunty umbrellas are arranged over footpath tables outside every eatery and bar.

The lovely streets are filled day and night with young, old and in-between people of all shapes, heights, sizes and nationalities—attractive Italians, affluent Germans, loud Americans, curious English and a fair share of stand-out Australians. Beautiful shops are full of seductive summer clothes, lacy lingerie, sexy swimwear, outrageously expensive handbags and the sexiest shoes to ever appear on the planet. The cafés and bars lining the harbour are packed past capacity with people enjoying the whole hedonistic scene. Along the beachfront are long rows of chirpy red-and-white-striped bathing boxes with geranium-filled baskets strung on the doors. They are so cheerful they make me want to run along the street singing 'Volare' or 'That's Amore', and I would, too, if I knew the words. The marina is crammed with luxurious yachts, all gleaming affluently in the sunshine. It's fabulous.

I want to be an Italian, an elegant signora. I want to live in Santa Margherita forever and have the owner of the most prized yacht—a suave and striking Italian man whose sole purpose in life is to dance attention on me—sail me around the Italian coastline while plying me with champagne and proposition. And that's as far as I will go with that little fantasy, I promise. You definitely do not want to hear the rest of it because the man is rampant and insatiable and … okay, okay, I'll stop.

Away from the tourist charm of the harbour, there are dozens of narrow cobblestoned streets branching out in several directions. Tall pink and yellow buildings with green shutters line these streets and, below, more gorgeous shops, lively cafés, busy restaurants and gourmet food shops abound.

In a cobblestoned *piazza* just behind the seafront stands a small church of such prosperity it takes our breath away upon entry. Charlie brings us here before we have even unpacked and settled into our apartment because he loves it so much and can't wait to show it off. The church seems a world away from the hot crush of the harbour.

Charlie relates its history in detail, but I can't remember it all now because of the brain cells I damaged one New Year's Eve in the late seventies, so you are now spared too much detail. But I do know that the church is about two hundred years old and was built by the villagers.

'Santa Margherita was a modest fishing village', Charlie tells us. 'But even the poor people saved their money and put it into the church, because the Italians love churches. This is really just a very small parish church.'

Parish church it may be, but inside is awe-inspiring opulence. A dozen chandeliers twinkle expensively and all wall space is covered with vivid frescoes. Imposing marble columns reach up to the frescoed ceiling and the altar gleams with gold icons and flickering candles. The atmosphere is cool, hushed; we whisper then sit quietly for a while to study the walls and ceiling. We watch as people come in to genuflect, cross themselves and sit and pray; to see this glittering showpiece used for its intended religious purpose makes all the richness seem somehow humble.

Back at the apartment, Geoffrey and I explore. It is on the sixth floor and has two bedrooms, a lounge room, a dining area, a modern kitchen and a gleaming bathroom. We feel obliged to remove our shoes as we enter, as the apartment is a place of typical Italian good taste, with shining polished floors in the lounge and dining rooms and plenty of marble in the bathroom and kitchen. A sunny balcony looks across to similar apartments and down the six levels below into one of those moody narrow cobblestoned streets. Across the narrow chasm from our balcony we can—if we want to—catch enticing glimpses into the living rooms and bedrooms of other apartments, and who knows, a voyeuristic moment might creep upon us, but for now there is too much else to capture our attention. If we look sideways from our long balcony we can see an inviting patch of blue sea and, beyond, lofty green mountains with villas and homes spilling downwards to the sea.

'It is nice; very Italian, isn't it?' Eva says of the apartment. We give her a quick hug because we know that without her and

Charlie's generosity, there is no way we would be in such a place. They rent this apartment from an Italian family who has owned it for generations and leases it out only after lengthy negotiations and extensive research into prospective tenants' backgrounds.

There are just two more days until Charlie and Eva leave. We're wallowing in their hospitality, making the most of every minute of their company. They lead us through the sunny streets in the mornings for coffee at lively cafés, and then take us to study and read aloud the timetables at the bus stop, the train station and the ferry terminal. Like parents about to leave children for their first day at school, they give us advice on how to get ourselves around once they are gone. In packed restaurants, they speak confidently to the flustered maître d and within minutes a table has been found, cleared and made up for us. They order pastas, salads and pizzas, ask for the red wine to be chilled, query the bill if necessary, while we sit back and let it all happen. It is all very pleasant and being looked after gives us a glimpse of what it will be like when we really are old and doddery and being led around, having menus and bus timetables read to us and food spoon-fed to us.

Charlie has a friend named Hugo who owns a popular restaurant in Sestri Levante, about a fifteen-minute drive south along the coast. Hugo is a gourmet chef and a fresco addict. When he isn't cooking in his packed restaurant, he scours the country, seeking out obscure towns with small churches that house little-known frescoes. Finding, examining and recording a new fresco is as thrilling to Hugo as perfecting a dish of *cozze alla marinara* (mussels in seafood sauce), of which he is a maestro. Charlie admires Hugo very much and must take us to him and introduce us to his food, his hobby and his big personality. This is another small and pleasurable adventure that requires nothing more from us than sitting in the back seat and being happily led along.

It is late on a Sunday afternoon and Sestri Levante is clogged with families and tourists. Another seaside resort town of irresistible charm, grand hotels and pricey shoe shops, Sestri Levante sits on a thin peninsula that cuts through the blue sea on either side. Small wooden fishing boats are scattered all over the tiny beach, which is surrounded by the same style of colourful, green-shuttered buildings we found in Santa Margherita. The narrow streets are packed with people and we are forced to shuffle along, shoulder to shoulder, compressed into our tiny bit of space, with no choice but to go with the crowd.

Earlier, Eva and I had risked our lives for a car space. We had circled the streets and public car parks with our heads out of the windows like curious dogs, anxiously searching for a space. After countless circles, we saw a large family packing into a car, ready to leave. Kids, buckets, spades and all the other beach equipment were being piled slowly and noisily into the car. Unfortunately, we were at the wrong end of a one-way lane heading out of the car park when we spotted the space behind us. A car coming down the right way had also observed the departing family. But we were there first and, even though we were heading out, the space was ours and nothing (and nobody) was going to take it from us. Eva leapt out of the car and ran back to the family (still busy packing kids and beach junk), to stand and guard the spot the second they vacated it. I followed, with the girlie belief that we would have more chance of holding our ground than our men, who were sitting nervously in the car. The retreating family took its time, brushing sand off the kids, changing clothes, looking for some stray bit of beach equipment. The other car sat menacingly. Charlie backed up, ready to manoeuvre into the park the moment the family car inched out. Finally the family appeared ready. Eva and I linked arms and stood in the middle of the lane, our brave backs to our adversary—if he wanted this space he was going to have to run us over, and we were not at all certain that he wouldn't.

Angry words spewed from the opposing car; Eva refused to translate. We could feel the fury. But as the family pulled out, Charlie backed in and there was nothing our rival could do about it. We had won this small but important battle for the car space and were ridiculously elated. We locked the car with exuberant spirits and almost skipped along on our way.

Car parks, or the lack of them, are the enemy of tourists in any place that it is desirable to visit all over the world. We can remember back to the late sixties and early seventies when tourism was a relatively small industry in Europe, yet parking was a major problem even then. It was the only time that Geoffrey and I rejoiced in touring on a motorbike. We used to giggle with glee at lines of cars searching for places as we sped past to wedge our way into slim spots between cars. It made up for all the times cars would rush pass us on wet winding roads, occupants serene and perfectly coiffured while we were stung in the face by sharp needles of rain and blown through to the bone by chilling winds.

It is too early to eat in Hugo's restaurant, so we shuffle with the other tourists through the clogged streets and then take refuge for thirty minutes in a sumptuous hotel lobby beneath a chandelier so elaborate we feel compelled to take photos of ourselves beneath it. Later, we sit for *aperitivi* in a small beachfront café and take our time over Campari-and-sodas. Charlie pays and asks for a receipt, which is reluctantly given. He tells us that some Italian café owners do not declare all their takings and pocket the black money. (Really? How unusual.) But in Italy it is us, the customer, who will be fined if the police catch us leaving a café without a receipt. I find it hard to believe that Italian policemen have nothing better to do than lurk outside cafés waiting for people to finish their Camparis, but apparently, on occasion, they do not.

It is now time to go to see Hugo, but first we must contemplate the clogged streets again, for Hugo's restaurant is right in the middle of the most congested of them all. We shamble along, crushed, claustrophobic, frustrated, until finally we find Hugo's place. We try to make a dignified exit from the crush, but are catapulted messily through Hugo's door. We step down into a cool, cavernous restaurant and walk past an open kitchen filled with perspiring chefs and a gas-type burner on which sits the biggest, flattest, widest frying pan I've ever seen. We go down a few more steps and into a large dining area lined with white wall tiles. Long wooden tables and benches require us to sit with strangers, all part of the experience because strangers quickly become friends after carafes of Hugo's red Ligurian wine are delivered to the table. The menu is written on a blackboard and we can order from that or go with whatever comes out of Hugo's kitchen; we choose the latter. We begin with *antipasti*: a simple dish of prosciutto and melon and a squid salad doused with Ligurian olive oil. Next, spaghetti with Hugo's pesto, which is bright green and a richer, creamier version than ours. The place fills up. We are joined at our long table by several young couples who immediately light cigarettes. We will never get used to this heavy smoking in public places; we hate it, but accept it as part of the European experience. More wine comes out and Charlie tells us that it is time for the *carne* (meat) course. This is something we are nonplussed by. Italians, we have discovered, eat their meat with nothing else. At Hugo's it is presented—a whole 900 grams of it—with nothing more than a wedge of lemon and a saltshaker.

'Outstanding', Charlie says as he squeezes lemon juice all over his steak and begins to wade through the great slab of meat with a mountain of enthusiasm and a pinch of salt.

'Aren't you going to have potatoes or vegetables or anything with it, a sauce perhaps?' I ask.

'It is not necessary', he says and dips his head back to the meat.

By now the place is wonderfully rowdy with families, kids and couples, all sitting at the big tables. Hugo, a squat, jolly man, finally comes out of the kitchen wearing a soaked jacket and a wet blue bandana and bearing a large bowl of mussels topped with breadcrumbs in a thick tomato sauce. He sits with us, invites us to dip chunks of crusty bread into the mussels and sauce. He has no English, but is very friendly through Charlie's translations.

We congratulate him on the food, his successful *ristorante*, but it is neither his food nor his *ristorante* he wants to talk about; it is his beloved frescoes. He tells Charlie and Eva of his latest discovery; an Umbrian town, a small church, a faded fresco. Only he and the locals seem to know about it. He smacks his fingers to his lips and rolls his eyes in pleasurable memory of the discovery. He will take a four-month break when the tourist season finishes and go on a countrywide fresco hunt. His mission, and he will not rest until it is accomplished, is to gaze upon and get to know every fresco on every wall in Italy. There must be hundreds of thousands. The thought exhausts us.

Later, as he leads us out with much hugging and back-slapping, he invites us to take a slice of *farinata*, a flat pizza-shaped chickpea-and-flour thing cooked in olive oil in the giant frying pan we saw on the way in. It is sliced into wedges and served with lemon, and is a specialty of the area, made all the more marvellous and tasty for its enormous presentation.

Charlie and Eva leave Santa Margherita after hugs and three-cheek kisses and promises to do this again next year. Their departure means that we can no longer put off going to Genoa to pick up the hire car. The train journey is surprisingly pleasant, taking us through a series of small towns and giving inviting glimpses of beaches packed with deck chairs and bronzed people. Rocky cliffs lead down to clear water and everywhere we look, purple bougainvillea grows—up walls, along fences, around gates; it even brightens up the train stations. Pots of geraniums, impatiens and petunias flourish in doorways, on balconies and on top of fences and gateways. Anywhere the Italians could put a pot of plants, they have, and I could kiss every one of them who went to the effort. They make a train journey behind their homes—something that could be dreary and dull—a heart-warming experience.

It takes an age to find the car-hire depot. Genoa's street-numbering system seems deliberately confusing. We start at number 18 and instantly come across number 157. Crossing the wide streets is terrifying. The Vespas line up at traffic lights like chariots about to roar into the Colosseum, their drivers resembling Russell Crowe on one of his most spirited days. We feel old and vulnerable. As if this isn't miserable enough, we then sink into feelings of guilt because we know we should spend time in Genoa, exploring the dark and narrow streets of the old quarter, admiring the stately buildings, seeking out the palaces and churches and lovely courtyards hiding behind old walls.

We vaguely know that Genoa is the city where Christopher Columbus was born. We really should find out if there is a Christopher Columbus museum, learn about his seafaring days in the fifteenth century, study Genoa's heroic sea-going past. We know we are lucky to be in Genoa and there is a rich history here, but right now all we care about is picking up the rotten car and getting the hell out of here.

By the time we actually get the car, our nerves are raw, and shatter further as we kangaroo-hop the car out of the bustle of Genoa. We miss the autostrada entrance (of course) that would lead us back to the relative safety of Santa Margherita within ten minutes and instead find ourselves on the pretty but frantic coastal road. We drive through busy little towns and streets so narrow I am terrified we will scrape the side of someone's house, tip over garbage bins, knock over babies in prams, squash scabby cats and amputate the legs of old men sitting in doorways.

Through the lovely little towns of Bogliasco, Sori, Recco and Camogli we fret and drive, with me shrieking and gasping at each near miss and Geoffrey responding in an ungentlemanly fashion. Finally, miraculously, we find ourselves back in the familiar and so-sweet streets of Santa Margherita.

Our god is being kind to us this day. He (although today I suspect He may be a She) has actually saved a parking spot for us in our street and, although it is about five centimetres too small for the car, Geoffrey (lovely boy) manages to reverse, straighten, go forward, reverse again, straighten again, go forward again several thousand times until he squeezes the car in. The process ages him ten years, but he does it. It is, however, clear that it will be impossible to get the car out of the tight fit ever again. And that suits me well.

'Leave it there forever', I tell Geoffrey. 'I hate it. We are not driving again, ever. And besides, we'll never find another place to park it.' And leave it we do. We check it every day to make sure it is all right and then leave it to the pigeons, which happily crap over it while we get to know the trains and buses pretty well for the rest of our time in Santa Margherita.

Back to my diary of 1970 I go, in search of any hint of us being nervous travelling along Europe's roads on the motorbike. There is not a single word to show how we felt about driving thousands of kilometres on a powerful motorbike virtually unprotected, for we had no leather jackets or pants or proper bikie gear. Of course, youth with all its confidence was on our side back then. I don't remember having a fearful day as we swerved around big trucks on highways, mounted city footpaths and thundered over mountain passes—apart from one, in Yugoslavia.

Yugoslavia was not a friendly place in those days, before it was cut up and turned into a confusing batch of other countries.

Crossing the mountains in what was then southern Yugoslavia was one of the most frightening days I can recall—because of the children. They stood at the side of the roads and for no reason we could think of other than that we were foreigners, threw rocks, stones and ugly curses at us. They spat viciously at the motorbike and, although small and mostly younger than twelve, had something malevolent about them. The stone-throwing and threats continued throughout a very long day as we travelled the twisting roads full of potholes and menace. Mostly the kids stood by the side of the road with piles of rocks at the ready, but some ran boldly in front of the bike, causing us to swerve dangerously and almost overturn.

As the day wore on it became more and more frightening, until we were both beside ourselves with fear, unsure of what to do. Each village seemed to hiss with unfriendliness. Stopping was out of the question. At the campsite the night before, we had heard horrible stories of people being robbed and beaten during rest breaks, of wallets and bags stolen during toilet stops. The stories gathered momentum as the night wore on and the cheap wine kicked in until we were convinced that if we stopped for even a minute we would be murdered, our bodies left to rot by the side of the road. We had been in Yugoslavia for about a week and had tried to love it, but it was impossible.

In Split on the Adriatic coast, we found some fun and liveliness, but on the drives through the countryside, we encountered nothing but hostility. In one place I waited and waited in a roadside store to buy a loaf of bread while the shopkeeper chatted grimly to the only other customer, without serving her. After ignoring me for forty-five minutes, they began sniggering in my direction, obviously talking about me with no intention of serving me. I left without the bread, but with a horrible feeling she had won some kind of unspoken but important battle. The incident was not a big deal, but was so overt it stayed with me all these years. (Nothing of it was recorded in my 1970 diary, naturally.)

We spend hours wandering around the waterfront in Santa Margherita, sitting on the sea wall and gazing out at the lavish yachts, me adding to my fantasy. Geoffrey is probably having the same one, swapping my handsome Italian man for a sultry Italian beauty with fleshy buttocks, but we never discuss our fantasies together (it is wise not to go down that path). Eva has told us that these yachts hardly ever leave the harbour; perhaps only once or twice a year. They certainly all look empty. Some have handymen on board, polishing already spotless chrome rails or hosing down clean decks, but most appear to sit alone, waiting for their rich owners to bestow a favoured visit on them.

We drink gin-and-tonics in a particularly buzzy bar and eaves-drop on conversations at nearby tables. Young attractive English girls on a three-day mini-break from high-powered jobs in London chat to young attractive German guys on a three-day mini-break from high-powered jobs in Düsseldorf. We become resentful of the ease with which these people can travel to Italy and the way they take it for granted, as well as their disregard for the healthy exchange rate their currencies give them. It seems that no matter where we live, the currency at the time is always at its lowest and the currencies of countries we want to travel to are enjoying a unprecedented buoyancy. When Geoffrey and I made the decision to leave England in the 1970s and sell our gorgeous little apartment in Southampton (where we had spent blissful years trying very hard to make babies every night), the pound was at a fairly good exchange rate. But as luck would have it (or would not have it, actually), the Australian government of the time decided to re-value the dollar, just about the time we were mid-air en route to a new life in Australia. With the stroke of an announcement, our entire life's fortune diminished to almost nothing. But hey, why am I complaining now about the pathetic Aussie dollar? We could have had our life savings in the South African rand or Polish zloty.

We order more gin-and-tonics to appease our jealousy of the lucky English and Germans, and make dinner plans.

We decide on Gemma, one of the most popular and least expensive cafés on the seafront. Goodness knows how many tables it turns over on a busy night. The moment customers finish and begin scraping their chairs back, a small team of waiters swoops in to clear plates, whip off stained tablecloths, lay down pristine new ones and plop down baskets of *grissini*. In less than a minute the table is ready for a new batch of customers. If it happens to be a group of eight for a table for four, no matter; another table appears from nowhere and is carried on top of a waiter's head before being joined onto the existing one while people at other tables happily squeeze out of the way to make room. Out comes another tablecloth from thin air, more *grissini* is pulled from behind someone's ear, chairs appear from a magic hat and Roberto is your uncle. After much shuffling and scraping and many *scusi*s and *mi dispiace*s, everyone is happy. It's quite wonderful.

This night we arrive late, because we want to sit leisurely and hang onto our table. We linger over Gemma's specialty, a simple spaghetti dish made rich by a mountain of parmesan and truckload of butter. We follow it with a thin-crusted pizza with nothing more than a tomato-and-mozzarella topping. We know this is the way a pizza should be, but it's very light on top and we wonder what Gemma's chef would think of some of our Australian pizza toppings. The Thai green chicken curry pizza might confuse him, and he'd probably roll his eyes with horror at a popular one in Noosa at the moment—a roast lamb dinner pizza, complete with roast pumpkin and minted peas.

We sit on, taking our time over the house wine—a bright yellow liquid in a small carafe with a head more like that on a beer than a wine—which is surprisingly good and pleasingly cheap. The whole scene radiates with happiness. We watch the changing procession of customers, stare down waiters anxious for our table and order more wine.

Late at night as the restaurant slowly empties, an attractive but sad-looking man comes in alone, takes a seat and orders a coffee. He is obviously well known to the waiters, who greet him warmly. He stares forlornly into space, smoking and stirring his coffee. After a few minutes his stare becomes heartbreakingly tragic and he then holds his head in his hands and weeps copiously. I am seething with curiosity and appear to be the only one taking any notice of him.

The man buries his face in his serviette and continues sobbing. I want to go and speak to him, console him, offer him my body for comfort (he *was* attractive), but Geoffrey isn't keen on the idea. 'Leave him alone', he says. 'Don't you dare go over to him. Don't even think about it.'

The waiters don't seem to notice the man's misfortune at all. Perhaps he does this often. I long to know what is wrong. A callous jilting? An unrequited love? A Mafia debt? A concrete-boot threat? Then it occurs to me—he probably can't find a parking space.

Five

Like everyone who travels to Italy, we want to experience the food. My interest in food is obsessive, I know. It comes before everything else, as evidenced by my time as a young woman living with a family in London in the swinging sixties. I missed the entire groovy London scene. Instead of going out each night to take part in love-ins and other orgies, I raced home from work to gorge myself on newfound English dishes with wonderfully suggestive names such as 'toad-in-the-hole' and 'spotted dick'.

Now, in Italy, I want the real thing, cooked by a mamma in a family-style *trattoria*. We don't hold much hope of finding one in a town as touristy as Santa Margherita, but the locals love to eat, don't they? They shun overpriced tourist traps, surely? There must be family-run places close by. There has to be a non-English-speaking mamma out there running a frantic but efficient kitchen while her good-looking sons serve the tables and her toothless old husband washes the dishes. Our delight is immense at stumbling—literally, for we have been on a late-afternoon walk and climbed up a track of more than five hundred steep steps—into a rough and rustic *trattoria*. It has everything we want: grubby plastic chairs under old and twisted olive trees, thriving red geraniums in empty paint cans, a messy courtyard, a couple of surly cats and a mangy dog. The views over the blue harbour of Santa Margherita and the green-and-purple-villa-dotted hills are breathtaking. And there is our mamma, plump and stern with a shabby apron and headscarf and not a word of English. She is perfect.

On a terraced section of the hill immediately below us, her vegetable garden flourishes with rows of red tomatoes, green beans, yellow peppers, shiny eggplants and healthy basil. Next to this is a small orchard full of prospering lemon and mandarin trees and heavily laden plum and apricot trees. Our hearts sing.

'A drink?' we indicate to her with sign language. It is very hot and there is no-one else around. We take refuge from the sun under the olive trees and drink gin-and-tonics and tell her, with much ridiculous hand signalling, that we will be back tomorrow night for a long and prodigious dinner. We finish the drinks and continue our walk, feeling a great sense of achievement.

Certain we will be surrounded by tribes of noisy locals joyously eating the best food in Italy, we arrive the next night to find the place completely empty. After a swollen-bellied waiter (mamma's husband, we assume) sits us down, he immediately tells us, with a bit of English, not to order *antipasti*, because there aren't any.

'What about those fat red tomatoes and all that fabulous basil right down there?' we ask and point to the thriving garden.

'No, no, no.' The vegetable garden and the orchard belong to the neighbour. Our disappointment is acute, but he does not appear to notice it.

'*Inglese?*' he asks us. No, no. Australian. What a coincidence. Do we know his cousin in Sydney? A *bella signorina*.

We tell him we don't but, so as not to disappoint him, we say we will look her up on our return. Off he trots excitedly to the kitchen to get, not trays of mamma's delicious food as we hope, but his cousin's Sydney address. We listen patiently to long stories told charade-style about his cousin and her Australian antics and finally plead with him for some food. Back he comes with small bowls of fat slabs of lasagne-like pasta, roughly cut into triangles and swimming in an oily ocean of dark green pesto, along with a plate of teeth-breaking bread. We eat cautiously, testing for broken fillings. Still no other customers come.

A young man in a pair of the brightest-possible pink shorts and a tiny apron (shorter than his shorts) comes out of the kitchen and announces that he will cook us a seafood feast in his smokehouse, a small wooden building from which an alarming amount of dark smoke billows our way. We sit over a small jug of the not-too-bad house wine and stare through the smoke to the gorgeous views until, without warning, our fat waiter marches over to our table, thumps his pasta-swollen belly and announces that it (the belly) will disappear on 15 September.

'What happens on 15 September?' we inquire politely, trying hard not to stare at the enormous stomach resting on our table. 'Is it some mystical Italian festival day when everyone's fat magically melts away?' If this is the case it will be more than worth the expense of a trip to Italy every September.

'No, it's the end of summer, when I stop drinking beer and the belly goes away', he announces, giving the gut another thump before disappearing happily off into the thick smoke. Ten minutes later he proudly brings a small plate on which sits a whole but tiny salt-crusted burnt fish, three large prawns and three scrawny crustacean thingies.

While it lacks some of the flamboyance we expected, we are determined to enjoy it, and dig in. Once the disproportionately large heads come off the prawns, we are left with exactly one fork-prong full of meat. The other unidentifiable things are so skinny they offer up a mere toothpick-jab of meat. Add to this the few bites of burnt fish, and there is our seafood extravaganza—a meal that takes, oh, a whole three minutes to eat and leaves our stomachs as empty as the restaurant around us.

We sip more wine and stare down through the smoke to the neighbour's vegie patch. Finally, mamma shuffles out of the kitchen, grubby, sweaty and apparently exhausted, which, when you consider her lack of cooking, is somewhat surprising.

'So, this is your wife?' we ask our soon-to-be-slim waiter. He is deeply shocked by the assumption.

'No, no, *no!*' he shouts. 'She just works here, does the dishes', and with that he presents us with a bill for the equivalent of one hundred and eight dollars. We pay it quickly and tip him generously, because we know this evening has taught us a much-needed lesson in the stupidity of stereotyping people. We laugh all the way down the five hundred steps and back to our apartment.

A small *panetteria* at the end of our street becomes our first outing each morning. The pastries and bread and pizza slices look quite different from those in our bakeries at home, but we are determined not to compare. If we want Australian pastries and giant seafood platters then we must stay at home. We hate whingeing tourists and are so frightened of becoming them we have vowed to slap each other around the ears each time we are caught comparing or complaining.

We know we are in a tourist town, but we also know there are dishes out there to be discovered and if we weren't so damned frightened of driving the car, we'd be heading off into country villages to find them. Out there are guinea hens with fennel, braised quail with juniper berries, and pot-roasted rabbit with chestnuts, all just waiting for us. Maybe we will find them; we have many weeks ahead of us.

The staff at the *panetteria* are not very friendly. I suspect they can't be bothered with my twangy Australian accent and lack of attempts to say anything at all in Italian. Every morning I wait patiently to be served while a non-stop line-up of vocal locals shout and brandish numbered tickets and jump ahead of me. It takes me three days to discover the ticket machine is outside the building, almost around the corner, nearly up another street. But by then one of the girls has softened towards me and even offers a shy smile. The next day I burst in boldly with my ticket and say '*due panini, per favore*', and she actually smiles brightly.

Obviously assuming I have taken a crash course in Italian and become fluent overnight, she reaches for two bread rolls and launches into a long babble of fast Italian. On and on she talks and for all I know she could be telling me juicy secrets about her most intimate sexual desires. But then again, she could be pouring out her life's woes, because to me all Italians sound the same whether they are deliriously happy or wretched with grief. I nod at her a lot and try to arrange my features into something I think is a cross between an interested smile and a sympathetic expression, then race home with my two bread rolls.

Geoffrey and I decide to walk to Rapallo, about three kilometres away. After checking to see that it really is our hire car hiding under the mountain of pigeon poop—and that it is still hopelessly jammed in with not much likelihood of being stolen because no thief could get in unless he was prepared to cut a hole in the messy roof—we set off happily on foot.

This is a lovely winding walk along the spectacular coastal front. Most of the walk can be taken along footpaths, which is fortunate because trucks, motor scooters, cars and those buzzy little three-wheeled Ape truck-things come shooting around corners and down hills at great speeds.

We pass sumptuous villas with curved bougainvillea-lined drive-ways and groomed grounds hanging out over the cliffs to the sea. One has a Rolls Royce parked casually near the front door and we stop to gaze longingly, both lost in private thoughts; me imagining it is my Italian yacht owner who owns this house and that I am in there right now stretching out on his sunlit balcony. Geoffrey, no doubt, is immersed in his own fantasy ... probably in the bubbling spa bath washing the silky arms of his lusty Italian beauty. We walk on until the footpath ends, then have to take to a wall-lined section of the road and once again take our lives in our hands because the road is narrow and the traffic is thick. We press our backs to ivy-lined walls as the traffic whooshes past, the drivers cursing our stupidity for being on foot on such a dangerous stretch.

This Ligurian coast is all too beguiling. I could exhaust my vocabulary of adjectives trying to describe the loveliness of the hotels and restaurants, the endless displays of flowers in planter boxes, yet more sumptuous yachts, the inviting beaches. The only jarring factor is the large number of rotund tourists hanging over sun lounges everywhere—but as I am usually one of them, I will not throw stones.

Charlie has told us about Rapallo, how it came to fame after World War I when it was the site of a European peace conference. It then became a favourite retreat for the English gentry, and evidence of their long-ago patronage lies in Rapallo's many old sprawling hotels. These hotels are faded places now, but were obviously once institutions of great self-satisfied glory—we can well imagine pseudo-royalty mingling with the boys from the polo club in the bar, while Camilla Parker-Bowles's mother sipped milky tea from a Royal Doulton teacup in the dining room.

We wander Rapallo's charming backstreets, stopping to look at the food shops with windows full of giant hams that we normally only ever see at Christmas and wheels of cheese as big as my spare tyre. I have always loved looking in gourmet food shops. I could never tire of stepping inside small dark delis where the owner peers out at me from behind a curtain of fat salamis and gives me a taste of his newest pungent cheese or invites me to sample his wife's latest batch of fig jam. We are sadly lacking in these shops in Queensland. I must make all my deli purchases from an acne-ridden schoolboy at the supermarket who always looks at me in a baffled manner, as though I have just arrived from another planet, when I ask for gorgonzola. I don't dare try him on the pecorino.

Back in Santa Margherita I set off to explore the backstreets on my own because I want to take my time in the food shops. There is one I particularly like. In its windows are shelves with big fishbowl jars full of creamy pesto, and I'd like to know how that pale green creamy look is achieved and why it differs from the dark-green oily pesto I thought came from Liguria, but the owner doesn't speak English, so I am left to wonder. The rest of the window space is filled with big dishes of octopus and chickpea salads, slabs of yellow frittatas dotted with bits of red capsicum, and giant platters of chargrilled eggplant floating in olive oil. I am enchanted and find myself staring thoughtfully at these treasures much like other women do at the baubles in jeweller's windows. I can find more beauty in a big dish of *parmigiana di melanzane* (eggplant with parmesan) than I could in a display of diamond rings. Geoffrey really is most fortunate to have me, and I'll remind him most forcefully of this immediately upon my return.

I buy the creamy pesto, fresh spaghetti, prosciutto and bread and head down the road to the cake shops. I have stood outside these windows before, admiring the *Torta della Nonna* (Nanna's cake) and the *Torta di Limoni*, a lovely lemon tart dusted with icing sugar. I buy half the Nanna's cake and then wander with my packages into another gourmet deli/wine/food shop. I try to tell the young man behind the counter that I want my chunk of parmesan grated, but he doesn't understand a word of English. Although the shop is full, no-one comes to our rescue, so I imitate a grating action and he beams and presses a large chunk of parmesan through a machine before presenting me with powdery cheese. We are both ridiculously pleased to have understood each other over something so simple as parmesan. I buy gorgonzola next, as well as bright red tomatoes with their vines attached and yet another large bottle of olive oil (we have taken to splashing it over everything and putting small bowls of it on the lunch table to dip our crusty bread into). Into the wine section I wander and wish we had these civilised shops in Australia where you can match a wine immediately to your purchases under the same roof, in the next aisle. It is just so damned continental.

I am thrilled with my small shopping expedition. For a few hours I have felt like an Italian and have convinced myself that I could easily slot into this lifestyle permanently. A few years of living here and I would be every bit as Italian as the Italians.

Although there are times when I still feel like an English person, I spent my formative years in Australia, surrounded by Italians. Their language was all around me in my growing years and some aspects of their lifestyle now seem as familiar to me as my own.

My parents were ten-pound Poms, part of the 1950s Australian immigration flood. They took their four kids on a very slow boat from England to Australia and settled in Melbourne's western suburbs along with thousands of European immigrants in a place named Sunshine. I doubt few places in the world have ever been so inappropriately named; there was nothing sunny about Sunshine. The mostly undeveloped landscape was flat and boring and uninspiring in every way imaginable.

In the 1950s, immigration was not quite as trendy and exciting as it is today. Sunshine was a hotchpotch of different nationalities, a cauldron of multiculture bubbling with Greeks, Maltese, Yugoslavs, Cypriots and Italians and a sprinkling of English and Scottish. In our street—in which the majority of people lived in dilapidated caravans on their blocks of land bought for about fifty pounds (the land, not the caravan) and the more well-to-do ones lived in half a house, literally—we were one of only two English-speaking families.

Many of the Italians used their front gardens to grow fruit and vegetables. They started with tomatoes, potatoes and beans and moved onto foods we had never encountered: red and green peppers, okra and zucchini (you must bear in mind that we were accustomed to dinners of mince and mashed potatoes with the occasional bean and brussel sprout thrown in for colour). Family members arrived from Italy to help with the vegetable production and later, when they had convinced us non-Europeans that these vegetables were indeed both edible and delicious, they began selling the vegetables at markets. Those same markets today, now with a strong Vietnamese influence, are a food lover's paradise and among the biggest and best in the Southern Hemisphere.

While the Italians and Cypriots grew vegies in their front gardens, the other locals found different ways to decorate. The Greeks erected stone statues and concrete paths, the English planted perfectly manicured lawns and lovely rose bushes, and some of the most creative Italians and Greeks who made an effort to embrace this strange new culture grew massive hedges and cut them into the shapes of kangaroos and emus.

What the Italians thought of Sunshine in the fifties and sixties could undoubtedly fill a very long book; back then, however, no-one in our sparkling social circle thought to ask them. We lived next door to a friendly Italian family but were too ignorant to bother giving a thought to any of the edifying things they had left behind—their thousands of years of rich history and fascinating culture, their strong family bonds and carefree lifestyles. That they might have visited churches and museums and gazed upon wondrous art in their home country (and might be missing these experiences) never occurred to us.

My father, always a bit of an entrepreneur, realised what was lacking in Sunshine: a delicatessen selling Italian food. He thought he would make a fortune, and he might have too if he had actually learnt what retailing was all about. He opened a shop and sold loose pasta from big perspex containers, olives and salty anchovies from large silver tins, never-ending cans of tomato paste, as well as ricotta, fetta and olive oil. Think about that. Can you imagine these products in Australia in the 1950s? They were as foreign to Australians as moon dust, and I can't say we embraced them in our own home either.

(Un)fortunately, our days as delicatessen owners were short-lived. My mother was less than enthusiastic about having to run the place while my father worked in a foundry, and things weren't much better when he took over on the weekends. He had no idea of the price of anything, so would take a stab, name a price and was obviously taken enormous advantage of. Everyone loved 'Mr Bob', as they called him, and so they should have considering he charged less for a product than it cost him to buy it.

When I went back to England in the sixties, the food had not changed much from when I left in my childhood, and thank goodness, too, for otherwise I never would have discovered the endless delight of the spotted dick. It is obviously only recently that the English have embraced exotic produce and realised that shiitake is not a swear word. I interviewed Jamie Oliver for my newspaper when he came to Noosa a few years ago, which wasn't easy, because all he wanted to do was exert his considerable charm and joke outrageously with the two hundred women who had flocked to the literary luncheon to see him. He said 'shag' a lot too, I remember, but when I did pin him down in a quiet corner, his passion for the pursuit of excellence in English food was very sincere. I also once interviewed the Two Fat Ladies—when there were still two—but their passion didn't shine. They were very intimidating, and I remember the dark one with the terrible black hair-dye job (Jennifer, I think, the one who no longer lives) ordering the 'filth' (instant coffee) to be taken from her hotel suite and replaced with the 'real' thing. But, I digress … this fat lady should move on to the next chapter.

Six

I really didn't mean to take you back to Australia, and to Sunshine of all places. Let's go somewhere especially nice in Italy now. Let's visit the Cinque Terre; that legendary rocky, rugged strip of coastline rising high out of the sea between Genoa and Pisa. Everyone knows about the Cinque Terre. We, of course, had never heard of it.

The young woman at the Santa Margherita information centre relieves us of our ignorance and says we can take the ferry around to one of the five villages comprising the Cinque Terre and then undertake one of the walks between villages. To walk between all five villages would be an impossible task—she doesn't actually say it, but the implication is clear—*for people our age*. We would need many, many hours and a high level of fitness, and there is not enough time left at ten o'clock on this sunny Sunday morning to do the Cinque Terre *properly*. For that, we would need to make an early start and allow ten hours or more (six for walking, the rest for exploring the villages). It is best to approach the Cinque Terre from the sea ... the views ... the cliffs ... *bello*. We can go and catch the ferry from Santa Margherita's harbour now. We do.

The ticket lady on the jetty ignores us along with the rest of the small crowd, preferring to talk on the telephone. Ten minutes go by. No-one knows what is happening and we all stand about worriedly, wanting to approach her, but she has her face buried in the telephone and will not look up to meet our eyes. This is something we have found often in Italy; queues going nowhere, ticket clerks who are either on the telephone or have no information, mild chaos at every train/bus/ferry/taxi station.

It is, of course, our own fault. If we had bothered to learn more than a sprinkling of the language before we came, we would at least have some confidence and could even attempt questions (and maybe understand some of the answers). As it is, we must stand in queues with other baffled non-Italian-speakers and wonder what the hell is going on.

After keeping us in the queue for twenty minutes, the ticket girl hangs up the telephone, comes out of her booth and tells us in English to go away, that the ferry will not be going today because the sea is too rough. We can see the sea is calm, flat and inviting, but obviously this has nothing to do with anything and we all shuffle off obediently.

We catch the train instead, planning to look at one, maybe two of the villages, as the day is now running out. From the north to the south the five villages of the Cinque Terre are Monterosso, Vernazza, Corniglia, Manarola and Riomaggiore. They all perch on cliffs overhanging the sea and are stunningly beautiful. It is as though Mother Nature threw a handful of gorgeous villages at a fertile cliff a few thousand years ago and then left them to do their own peaceful thing while time stood still around them.

It takes about an hour by train to get from Santa Margherita to the first village, and then about two minutes by train between villages, sometimes through short pitch-black tunnels.

We go to the southernmost village of Riomaggiore and spill out of the train with hundreds of other tourists. It is getting on for mid-day now and we are not prepared for anything more than a pleasant walk, so we head off along the romantically named *Via dell'Amore* (street of love) toward Manarola. The level, man-made path curves around the rocky cliff face and we walk briskly, passing ambling tourists, scoffing at the notion that this Cinque Terre walk would take six hours to complete. We have not given Riomaggiore a moment's look, so keen are we to see what this walk is all about, worried that the day will run out on us. Now, as we approach Manarola after an easy twenty-minute walk, we are sorry we did not linger in Riomaggiore. This is easy, and the Cinque Terre bewitching.

Manarola—a jumbled cluster of ancient yellow, pink and grey stone houses built into the cliffs and spilling down to the sea—is far too enchanting to hurry through. Never before have we been confronted with such allure. Love at first sight really does happen, and we could happily find an Internet café and email back to Australia to tell the kids to sell our house, keep the money, impound the dog, forget those pleas to give us grandchildren ... we are never coming back.

We walk down the main street, an intriguing narrow pedestrian laneway that leads down to the sea and is lined with bursting cafés, busy shops and tiny bars. Manarola is packed with people eating, drinking, swimming, sunning, laughing and owning—for the afternoon—the most beautiful views imaginable. There is obviously no hope of getting a table in any of the restaurants or cafés for lunch, so we buy freshly baked focaccias filled with chargrilled eggplant and zucchini from a flustered baker who can barely keep up with demand.

Further down the narrow street we buy a bottle of local wine, *Vendemmia di Monterosso al Mare* (as my notes now tell me), at a shop filled with local wines and olive oil and jars of preserved lemons. The friendly girl happily uncorks the wine and gives us paper cups. Our love grows. We take our bounty down to the tiny habour and sit on the rock wall to further enjoy this daytrip to heaven. We eat. We drink. We sigh.

The cool green water is too tempting. We have no swimwear, just matching underwear for me (that *never* happens, lucky day) and navy blue underpants (that could, if you stretch the imagination, pass for Speedos) for Geoffrey.

We struggle self-consciously out of our outer clothing, but need not have worried. Not one of the hundreds of people splashing in the water, sunning on the rocks or sitting in boats and cafés is the slightest bit interested in us. Fifteen minutes of cool paradise in the water, another fifteen in the sun to dry off, and we are ready to tackle the walk to Corniglia. We can see it in the distance, resting on the top of a cliff looking out over the sparkling sea. Easy.

We walk and climb on a natural track past sweet peas and wild poppies until the path becomes rugged. On and on we climb, our cocky confidence from the previous walk seeping out of us with each step and cup of sweat. Still further we climb as the path gets steeper. The compelling views to the glorious sea below tempt us to fly off the cliffs, down into the deep water, and indeed, right now death is not a bad option—at least it would stop our thumping hearts.

We have not brought hats, sunscreen, insect repellent or proper walking shoes, but the grapevines and orange groves and unbearable beauty of these terraced hills help us forget we are wearing just shorts, sleeveless T-shirts and flimsy sandals. We manage to find a little more strength to go on. And on, and on, and on.

A strenuous, unforgettable hour later we stagger on shaking legs into Corniglia and fall into bottled water and love again. Once rested in the small, treed *piazza*, we explore Corniglia's enchanting streets, some so narrow that if we walk side by side our shoulders almost touch the buildings on each side. We walk through an arch leading to a small quadrangle, where yet another breathtaking view of the sapphire sea and towering distant cliffs stretches out before us. It is mid-afternoon by now, very hot and sunny, and Corniglia is beginning to quieten down, as sensible people take to their homes and hotels for siesta. But the bottled water, the view and the allure have rejuvenated us and we are ready for more. A sign tells us the next village, Vernazza, is an hour-and-a-half away.

'We could do it again, couldn't we?' Geoffrey says now that his belly is sloshing with water and his legs have stopped shaking.

'I don't know', I reply. My own belly is sloshing happily too, but an hour-and-a-half more of difficult climbing concerns me. 'It really is too beautiful to stop and go home now, though', I say before taking another swig of water and tramping on.

The track snakes in front of us for miles, we can see it slinking its way up the mountain. There are lovely houses up there, with grapevines growing in neat tumbles down the cliff and we want to get closer to them. Again we climb, up rocky steps carved into the mountain, some so steep we have to stop and hoist ourselves up, hands on knees, groans on lips. We can see fabulous yachts anchored in attractive little bays in the far distance below and can just make out tanned figures sitting elegantly on decks, no doubt drinking champagne and making plans for lovemaking and siesta. I am convinced not only that my fantasy man is down there, but that I should be on the yacht with him. In the still air high up on the cliffs, his self-satisfied voice wafts up into my seething imagination … 'Let me top up your champagne, you hotty.'

I curse him bitterly and hoist my aching bulk up another brutally steep step.

Finally we stagger into Vernazza, almost crying with relief. Later, when we have spent time in Vernazza and even later still, when we have left it, we will think back to that day, our first time there, and would gladly give up a year of our life to repeat the experience.

Vernazza is, like the other villages, very old and proud of its fishing traditions. It faces a tiny bay dominated by cliffs and two ancient towers and holds many mediaeval features, as well as a beautiful church built in the Gothic–Ligurian style in the early fourteenth century. We should explore it. A backpacker passing us on the track stopped and told us of it and urged us not to miss it. But it requires walking up yet more steps, so instead we head for a bar right on the water and down two gin-and-tonics each in four minutes. We cannot move. Our legs have turned to jelly, our backs ache, our feet are blistered. The waiter is obviously accustomed to this—unfit, unhealthy people lurching drunkenly into his bar from the surrounding cliffs—and nods understandingly when we request a third gin-and-tonic in a hurry.

We can catch the train back to Santa Margherita. We have done well, completed walks and seen four of the five villages—the girl at the information centre doubted we could manage one—and are justifiably proud of ourselves. But the clock in the beautiful old tower in the square tells us it is only 5.30 p.m., which means we have many hours of daylight left. We sip our third gin-and-tonic slowly, watch the people on the beach, gaze at the blue water, admire the little boats and look back to the busy square. We want more.

'How long does the walk to Monterosso take?' we ask our waiter.

'Where have you come from?' he asks in return.

'Vernazza, and it was bloody hard. It almost killed us.'

He nods again, then smiles. 'The next walk is almost exactly the same.'

Shit.

We are full of gin-and-tonic-induced bravery as we pack up our few belongings and walk through the lovely streets of Vernazza. The old multicoloured houses with washing flapping from the windows above are even more charming, if this is possible, than any we've seen before. We wander through a maze of narrow, bewildering streets, unable to find the signpost to Monterosso. We ask a German couple with two young daughters if they know where the track to Monterosso starts, and indeed they do. They are staying in an old stone house at the beginning of the track and will take us to it. The little girls are delighted to practise their English and chatter brightly to us as we make our way to the track. They tell us a man, a local they met on holiday here last year, offered to rent them his own home for the summer for about the equivalent of fifteen Australian dollars a day and they gratefully accepted. The house is built into the cliff and the family insists we come in and look. It is rustic and delightful with spectacular views worth $1500 a day. We wonder why we never meet people like that, willing to give their fabulous homes to strangers for a tiny fee.

The Germans know the area. They tell us the walk—this last bit to Monterosso—is at least a two-and-a-half-hour arduous climb. We want to cry, back down, turn back, but by now we have missed the last train from Vernazza and must go on, so we do our best to collect ourselves. We are brave but exhausted warriors. We will, we must, make it to the next stop.

Once again we climb and climb, the path becoming dangerously narrow and difficult in places, but the views more and more beautiful. We hike past jungles of wild flowers and olive and lemon groves, sometimes past villas high above us with grapevines and vegetable patches terracing their way down the mountain.

Sunburnt, sweating, bitten, panting and dribbling saliva, we continue. I fantasise about what would happen if I sprained an ankle here. How would I get out, down the cliff? 'You go on without me', I would say in the self-sacrificing manner of a mortally wounded John Wayne being pursued by frenzied scalp-hunting Indians. 'Leave the gun, tell mamma I love her. Now go ... just go.'

I am delirious of course. I push on, following Geoffrey's retreating bum in a stupor as he mounts steep steps much more easily than I can. People, sensible people with proper walking boots and hats, come downhill towards us, taking in our red balloon faces with undisguised pity.

'Is it all downhill for me going this way?' they ask.

'No', I lie because I can't bear their coolness, hate their comfortable boots and am envious of their protective hats. 'It starts to go up, very steeply.'

After what seems like more than two hours but is in fact just over one, we come across a levelled part (oh joy, oh thank you, thank you, hiking god), but then the path slopes frighteningly down, way, way down at a terrifyingly steep incline. We clamber down like goats on rickety legs and peer through the foliage. There are villas in the immediate distance and we want to cry out to the people in them to send doctors, stretchers, bottles of water—come and save us. And then, suddenly, we see a large and gorgeous hotel jutting out over the sea and a divided path forking off into two different directions. We take a right turn, the wrong one of course, and after fifteen difficult and wasted minutes, have to turn back. Another exhausted couple follow us and do not hide their annoyance when they too must turn back and climb again until they reach the right path.

We fall into Monterosso, vowing never to walk another inch again in our lives, and find ourselves in the middle of a huge party. The town is teeming with attractive people promenading along the waterfront wearing lovely bright clothes and eating *gelati*. Orange-and-white-striped umbrellas and blue deck chairs line the beach, and the cafés are filled with people drinking wine. We immediately perk up. We have an hour before the last train back to Santa Margherita and we want wine, we want rest, we want to soak up the atmosphere of this lovely place.

We have completed the Cinque Terre journey, the most spectacular walk we have ever done in our lives and we cannot wait to get back to that girl at the information centre in Santa Margherita to brag.

The following year, we return to the Cinque Terre, and this time we are sensible. We stay a night in Monterosso and a night in Riomaggiore. We want to get to know the area in a more relaxed way, without leaving behind several buckets of sweat.

Our hotel in Monterosso, Albergo Pasquale, is on the beachfront and has views resembling a life-sized postcard. We explore the promenade on steady legs soon after arriving fresh from the train. We are different people to those red sweaty walkers who crawled into the town at the end of the gruelling walk last year—we take our time exploring the beach, wander through the narrow laneways lined with old fishermen's houses, sip coffee in tiny cafés with rows of washing flapping above us. We are now ready to walk—mostly downhill—to Vernazza.

But what was uphill last year has miraculously changed and we are walking uphill once again. Did I imagine that climb last year? No, I did not; it's just that the track climbs, plunges, climbs and plunges again. It is difficult and challenging, but oh so wonderful. Hormonal teenage boys race past us in energetic droves on the high rocky parts, while we lurch and dribble and stop every few minutes to take photos and swigs of water. It seems as if this is the day chosen by every high school boy in France to come to Italy and do the Cinque Terre walk. We have hats and boots and sunscreen this time and are prepared and determined. We keep catching up to the schoolboys because they keep stopping—out of sight of their over-weight teacher who is steaming way behind them—to smoke. The little brats sit on the path, blocking our way, puffing frantically on as many cigarettes as they can fit in before the chubby teacher catches up. We step over them, only to have them charge past us in an energetic jumble of arms and legs a few minutes later, and then it is our turn to come across them smoking again. This little game goes on all the way to Vernazza.

Every shaky step we take past olive trees and lemon groves is rewarded with a view of breathtaking beauty. Coming into Vernazza from this direction is much better than from Monterosso. The water in Vernazza's tiny harbour is clear and green and from high up we can see the outlines of people stretched out, floating.

When we finally arrive at the harbour, we leap into the water with as much energy as the French schoolboys and splash around for an hour with young Italian women in micro-bikinis who look like they've stepped out of the pages of *Vogue* and fleshy mammas in billowing bathing suits who look like they have rarely stepped away from the dinner table.

This time in Vernazza we discover an amazing young man who waits tables at one of the cafés in the small square. He is tall and slender with tight buttocks and dark curly hair and big white teeth, and has a manner so charmingly Italian it is well worth travelling the 12 000-plus miles from Australia just for the pleasure of being served a bowl of spaghetti by him.

We watch him at work, going through the full range and virtuosity of his waiting skills. He greets each customer gallantly, flashing his lethal smile. He pours beers, brings pizzas and clears plates, all the while speaking English to everyone in his devastatingly sexy accent. I blatantly stare at this gorgeous man and give full flight to my fantasies as we loiter over lunch, staying long after everyone else has left and gone for siesta.

In Riomaggiore we stay the night at Villa Argentina, lusciously located on the terraced hills covered with flowers and looking out to clear blue skies. In the long evening we sit on the balcony and sip local wine and look at the view before wandering through the small town, where we eat an especially unsatisfactory meal in a crammed and smoky café. The staff refuse to accept credit cards, and Geoffrey is forced to run back up a stony flight of steps to the hotel for money.

The next day we take the train, intending to get out at the next stop, but the train sits at the end of a dark tunnel and we wait in darkness, not realising that this is actually our stop and we are supposed to get off in the tunnel and walk up to the station. We are dismayed when the train finally takes off and whizzes past our station and we are forced to sit on a long journey to a town we know nothing about. Instead of treating this as an exciting adventure, we carry on like wimps—well, truth be known, I do—and whinge throughout the long half-hour until the train stops and we are forced to get out, find another bored ticket seller, queue for thirty minutes to buy a ticket, get on another train and head back to the Cinque Terre.

Our mood is bleak when we arrive back at Monterosso and we somehow cannot get into the spirit again. We decide it is time to leave the Cinque Terre behind for perhaps another year, and head back to the station. By this time I am paranoid about getting on the wrong train and ask a group of stationmen who are sitting playing cards in a small room if we are on the right platform at least thirty times. Just as the announcement for the train to Santa Margherita begins, one of the men pokes his head out and tells me we are on the wrong platform; we need to be on number five, across the track, but must take the underground tunnel to get to it. I am determined not to miss this train and proceed to do something no woman over the age of fifty should ever do—I jump down onto the tracks and run across. Geoffrey follows suit. When we reach the other side and see the stationmen waving angrily at us, the reality of what we have just done hits me: *we ran across a railway track in front of an approaching train*. God, we are stupid. Don't tell my kids.

Seven

Noise, it has to be said, is something Italians love very much. These peaceful, fun-loving people embrace any kind of noise, as long as it is ear-splitting. There are, of course, good noises; the joyful sound of church bells ringing every half-hour in every Italian town and village ... the soothing sound of water splashing and flowing from fountains in every *piazza* all over the country ... the hissing of espresso machines ... the kitchen clatter that seems to leap out of every doorway in every street ... the high-pitched squeals of children playing on the beach. These are all part of the wonderful Italian approach to life, and very welcome noises they are, too. But then there are the other noises. So very many of them.

Our Santa Margherita apartment (are we still in Santa Margherita in chapter seven? Don't despair, we are heading to Capri soon; you're going to love it) is positioned to capture a whole gamut of noises. They fly out from every apartment as mammas shout at children and husbands, showers go at full belt, televisions blare out dramatic soap operas and game shows, babies cry, spaghetti boils and residents make lusty love (we are in Italy, what do you expect?). It all comes inside through our apartment windows and we love it.

But this is all mere background music to the constant cacophonous building noises that go on all day. Where you have beautiful, old buildings, you also have need for ongoing refurbishment, which means high-powered drills, nerve-grating grinders and ear-piercing cutters—all punctuated with Italian shouts and what we assume to be earthy obscenities, as machines break down and electric saws refuse to saw.

From the lush green villa-dotted hills in the distance comes a whole other set of noises. Whipper snippers (undoubtedly given a much more glamorous name in Italian) roar and electric olive-tree-pruners buzz as villa owners go about cleaning up their orchards and vegetable gardens, making the hills come alive with the sound of high-energy gardening. In the early morning hours—usually about four o'clock—the pigeons vocalise their wakefulness on every bit of available rooftop in town. Their sexy cooing is pleasant but doesn't quite go with the desire for lazy holiday sleep-ins. The pigeon choir is interrupted at about six o'clock by the garbage truck that thunders into the street below and spends a good fifteen minutes roaring and grunting as its automatic grabber lifts every overflowing (mostly with empty wine bottles, ours) garbage bin.

At ten o'clock one morning, just as we are enjoying a very Italian breakfast of bread, jam and strong black coffee amid a relatively peaceful background—just one tile cutter in action—an enormous water truck rumbles to a stop below us. A little man gets out, attaches a hose to the tank on the back of the truck and for the next long hour hoses down the street while the truck revs, roars, bellows and belches happily behind him. The jarring sounds bellow up the abyss between buildings and thump around our balcony. The next day, the truck comes back for another thunderous hour, right underneath our balcony again. Apparently our little man had done only half the street yesterday. So much noise for so little result.

Against this raucous background is the ceaseless revving of the ubiquitous Vespas. Surely every Italian man, woman and child rides a Vespa and loves to rev it powerfully at every corner of every street? But more about that later.

And this time of year—the middle of summer—is festival time. Italians love an outdoor stage with hugely amplified music and a never-ending line-up of would-be singers who perform off-key plaintive love songs, piercing the hot night air and encouraging every dog within hearing distance to raise its head to the moon and join in. (That last bit isn't actually true, but I thought it added a bit of colour to the story.) At the end of these festivals, usually well into the late night when we have at last drifted into a decent sleep, the fun-loving Italians finish the night off with clamorous fireworks displays.

Still, we consider ourselves lucky to be staying in a relatively quiet street. Yesterday we overheard a group of young Americans talking on the beach.

'What is it with these bells, man', one of them said as the clanging 12.30 p.m. show was in long, lovely session. (He really did say 'man', I'm not making that up.) 'They go on all day and night.'

His friend showed no sympathy. 'Our hotel is over a fish market', he replied. 'We have not slept one night the whole way through since we arrived, man.'

There are concerts being performed all over Italy during our stay. In Spoleto, some of the world's most famous voices have come out to perform including Placido Domingo and Luciano Pavarotti (although Pavarotti said he didn't feel well and went home).

We have not had the foresight to buy tickets, but one night we watch an outdoor concert on television, having no idea where it is being held, but it looks like the most romantic venue in the world. This is not a Pavarotti or Domingo concert; it appears to be a rock concert. We watch as a busty Italian beauty spilling out of a gorgeous white jacket hosts the long concert in an amphitheatre of such colossal size, the atmosphere (even sitting in our lounge room) is electrifying. As the summer evening closes in, the television cameras capture all the magnificence of the venue and the slowly changing sky. It is more beautiful than I can find words to describe it to you. There are hundreds of people in the amphitheatre and after each performance the cameras span back over the clapping crowds and soar up and out of the amphitheatre, high over the sky for a big and beautiful bird's-eye view. So much beauty, so much enjoyment; and this is not a crowd that has come out to see opera or a highbrow musical soirée, it is a young, hip crowd enjoying a rock concert in the most gorgeous of settings. Geri Halliwell comes out wearing a tiny white handkerchief and long white boots and sings 'Scream If You Want To Go Faster'. She looks fabulous and sexy in the moonlight and we enjoy her performance, and not just because she is the only performer we can understand.

We don't really need concerts in atmospheric amphitheatres when we have the daily theatre of Italy's streets before us. We can sit down at any café, order a coffee and let the passing parade put on the show. Babies and toddlers are given as much attention as adults when the Italians take to the streets, and rightly so. These little ones especially love the cocktail hour, when they sit on various relatives' knees and, while the grown-ups enjoy pink Campari cocktails, they gobble the olives that come out with each drink. We spend evening after evening watching parents and grandparents dote on their babies, feeding them the olives, mindful of the pips.

Italian babies also love Vespas and are, in true Italian style, encouraged to don a tiny helmet and scoot along on the driver's knee or, if at toddler stage, stand on the footplate, often with the family dog. Sometimes up to three children will stand on the front of a Vespa with their mamma and papà on the seat. It is positively charming. The Vespa cuts through all age groups; gorgeous young girls with strappy high heels and Prada handbags slung over slim shoulders whiz by, often overtaken by leathery old men in baggy pants and singlets. Bicycles are popular too, which is understandable when you consider how little parking space is available. It is not unusual to see an old woman in head-to-toe black peddling speedily by with shopping bags over both shoulders, often overtaking a young guy busy watching out for a *bella ragazza*.

One young enterprising couple gave new meaning to the word 'dink' (or whatever the Italian translation is). While he peddled, she sat on the handlebars facing him with one leg slung over his shoulder, the other around his waist. How he could see where he was going is anyone's guess, but I am sure that had we been able to see his face, it would have had a huge smile on it.

If watching Italians in the streets is fun, then watching them at the beach is better than a day at a theme park. Children are a joy to watch on any beach in the world; the blokes are interesting too, especially the old men in baggy pants on saggy deck chairs; but it is the women I really like to look at. Not the young beautiful bikini-clad things—they are lovely and sexy and best left for the young studs to ogle—I like to watch the exquisitely chubby mammas, and find them a never-ending source of theatre.

No self-respecting mamma—even if she does have the side effects of too many years of spaghetti carbonara hanging around her stomach and hips—will be prevented from struggling into a swimsuit to enjoy the beach if that is what she wants to do. She will let her stomach ripple down, her bum hang out and her thighs rub together as she claims a spot of the beach as her own, and no-one will think any less of her for it. She is the one I love best, completely unselfconscious and enjoying the beach just as much as the sexy slim girls; she is a woman to emulate.

I don't much care for the emaciated older women who have spent all of their summers lying in direct sunlight and now resemble dried raisins who could quite possibly survive an entire week without water in the Gobi desert. These women, many in their sixties and seventies, still lie with their faces directly in the sun even though they have no elasticity left in their skinny bodies. And why do they believe the topless look is still a good one for scrawny boobs that look like deflated balloons after a big New Year's Eve party? These dried-up, over-tanned, baked-black women have taken no heed of the cancer warnings and can be found on beaches all over Italy with their younger counterparts, who are well on their way to becoming the same. The Italians simply cannot resist the sun.

Sometimes the plump mammas come to the beach in small groups, without a swimsuit among them. Obviously there has not been an intention to swim, just a sit on the pebbles, a paddle by the edge, a gossip with friends. But as the sun wears them down, bits of clothing and inhibitions are abandoned. First off are the shoes and those attractive knee-high stockings. Wriggling bare toes by the edge of the water is one of life's small and free pleasures and it leads to more indulgence, so off comes the blouse. Beneath the blouse is usually a formidable garment of the corset kind that could pass for a beige or black swimsuit, so modesty remains intact. Voluminous skirts are shucked up around fleshy thighs and, after enjoying five minutes of splashing in the cool ankle-deep water, caution and ample bodies are thrown right into the deep of it. In they plunge, swimming, splashing, shrieking, laughing and having a bloody good time in corsets and skirts. I believe it is one of the best sights in all of Italy.

Mothers with sons are another source of amusement for me. We see many, for it is school holidays and they are out en masse. We have heard that Italian mothers like to look after their sons—to make their beds, cook, wash and iron for them, even long after they are grown men, married with sons of their own (no wonder Italian men love their mothers)—and we see nothing to contradict this.

Mamma arrives at the beach carrying the bags, beach mats, drinks, food, extra clothes (her sons must not be forced to sit around in wet swimmers for the journey home). The boys stand around, perving on the young girls, while Mamma carefully unpacks each item. They watch her brush pebbles and small rocks aside to make a soft space on which to unroll the beach mats. Never do we see young boys do this for themselves. When Mamma has made the patch as comfortable as she possibly can, her boys throw themselves down and she delves back into her bag and brings out towels to roll up as cushions for their teenage heads. Then she goes back into her bag and produces fruit juice and soft drinks for them, even putting the straws in the bottles. She then feeds them big filled *panini* and fusses while they eat. She watches, amused, as they pick up pebbles and throw them at each other. When they are ready to go into the water, only then does she look after herself.

All this we have observed on the tiny pebbled patches of free beach in Santa Margherita. There is, no doubt, a full program of riveting beach theatre at all the private beaches in front of those gorgeous striped bathing boxes, but we will never know for sure because we refuse, absolutely, to pay to sit on a beach.

For these past few weeks we have liked to think we have embraced Italian culture, but when it comes to paying for beach space, our inner Aussie rears up and objects loudly. It wants to shout, 'Strewth, stone the crows', but we don't normally speak in that ocker way, so instead we say, 'Fuck that for a joke'.

We believe that paying to sit on a beach is an affront to every-thing in us that is Australian. We know we would receive a deck chair, perhaps even a locker, and could change our clothes in one of those jaunty beach boxes, but *pay* to go onto a beach? It is out of the question.

So we sit squashed up with the other penny pinchers on the hard pebbles on the small free patch and gaze enviously at the paying people sprawled out on comfortable lounge beds next door. This beach snobbery doesn't stop on the pebbles, even the sea is sectioned off. The private beaches and hotels have their own bits of sea, but I'd like to know who says only those who pay to sit on a private beach or stay in a hotel can swim in a certain area of water. This apartheid of the ocean seems utterly stupid, yet all over the coast vast sections of the water are roped off. Only the free section is not roped off and it is very small.

I swim out deep in the pauper's water. I look across the ropes to where the privileged people swim and cannot work out why their bit of water should be different to mine. I can understand people collecting money on the beach if they provide deck chairs and lockers and cute beach huts, but dictating who can swim in which bit of water? It's absurd. I slip under the ropes and feel daring in the rich people's sea. I splash around, tread water and swim, certain that everyone can tell I am an interloper. What if the private beach or hotel police come to order me out? Surely no-one can monitor the ocean? I pee in their bit of water. It's a pathetic little protest and only I, surrounded for a few brief moments by warm water, know about it, but I feel a little less peeved by it all.

Although I envy the people who can sit in those striped beach boxes in Italy, I can also relate to them, because Geoffrey and I knew the pleasures of the beach box for a few years in Australia. When our children were young we used to holiday on the Mornington Peninsula in Victoria with another couple who had children the same age. We rented an old house with little sleep-out places in the garden to which we banished the children at an unfair early hour so we could get stuck into the wine cask. The house was high up on a hill and a short-but-steep-and-tricky journey down to the beach had to be undertaken each morning. The house came with a little beach hut on the sand, not gaily striped, but with a table and chairs and electricity, which meant a few comforts could come right down to the seaside with us.

With five children and four adults in the group, the amount of gear that went down the hill each day was considerable. First there were the banana lounges, broken things with rusty frames and loose plastic flappy bits. They had to be set up in precisely the right spot for us women—in the sun but with a bit of shade, out of the wind but with the chance of catching the cooling breezes, facing the water and not the bush behind us. There was much folding, unfolding, moving and grumbling from the men before they achieved the correct banana lounge positions to suit our many requirements. At this point, we would throw ourselves on the lounges and remain motionless for the rest of the day.

This was the first trip down the hill for the men. They then had to go back up for the sandwiches they had made before sunrise for the children's morning tea. Down the hill came a Tupperware container the size of a washing machine, filled with Vegemite sandwiches, and even though it was just nine in the morning the container had to be opened the minute it arrived, whereupon kids, dogs and seagulls appeared magically from behind bushes, out of the sky and from the water to squabble, fight and grab.

Three or four more trips were undertaken before we had everything necessary for a day at the beach, including blow-up toys, romance novels and the essential wine cask. Then came the grand finale, the last trip—and for the men the most important. They would take off with an excited spring their step, unlike the dragging listless efforts of before, because they were about to bring down the necessities for their day: a television and bar fridge.

After staggering down the hill with their precious cargo and setting up the fridge and television inside the beach hut, they would then sit outside on the tiny deck with their backs to the beach, beers in hand, peering inside the gloom of the hut to watch the cricket.

At the time we never considered this as the ultimate in stupid exercises, because every other man on the beach did the same. In fact, the beach was filled with men with their backs to the sea peering into dark beach huts. Come to think of it, it was also filled with women glued to banana lounges reading Jackie Collins novels.

Eight

Let us go now to Portofino, playground for rich and beautiful people and for a short while us, normally full card-carrying members of the hoi polloi. We can go by boat or walk there from Santa Margherita and, for a few hours, pretend we are part of the learjetting, yacht-sailing, highfalutin crowd.

Portofino is one of those places that reside in the part of my brain reserved for all my late-night holiday fantasies. I imagine I'll run into Liz Hurley there, all pouty lips and bare boobies, sunning herself on the deck of one of the yachts anchored in the harbour.

Portofino has been on top of my list of fantasy holiday destinations ever since I read an article slamming the place by an unctuous reviewer. He was staying at the fabulously famous and outrageously expensive Hotel Splendido, which sits high and haughty on the hill overlooking the tiny yacht-filled harbour.

The pretentious reviewer had visited the hotel for many years, but this particular year he was not happy. He was there with his photographer girlfriend—pretentious reviewers always have equally pretentious girlfriends who just happen to be photographers and so too get to go to lovely places and eat and drink for free—and his list of criticisms was endless.

He complained because his breakfast tray had contained little pats of butter wrapped in foil and his tea had come, not perfectly drawn and awaiting his pleasure in a Crown Derby pot, but in the form of an offensive tea bag sitting on a saucer.

'I was not put on this earth to fiddle with teabags', he wrote.

And, as if fiddling with teabags and opening one's own butter pats was not vexing enough, the Italian waiter who delivered the offending breakfast tray further insulted our reviewer by saying 'good evening' when it was actually morning. Horror. Obviously this lingual aficionado has never confused a *buon giorno* with a *buonasera* before. And then—complete disaster—the photographer girlfriend's cup had a 'serious' chip in it. The reviewer was so angered he went down to reception to find someone to complain to and, after bawling out some lackey, wandered into the dining room and out to the kitchen. Here he examined the plates (for further serious chips, true) and found them not warm enough (or something like that) and was further outraged ... and on and on the nitpicking review went.

Anyway, the point of my longwinded story is that the reviewer had his photographer girlfriend photograph him on the balcony, surrounded by the hotel staff, who obviously didn't know they were about to get a shitty review and were smiling happily, seemingly delighted to pose with him. These drop-dead gorgeous elegant Italian waiters in smart jackets and ties surrounded our reviewer, who was red-faced, flabby, sweating and dressed in a pair of shortie-pyjama-things. The backdrop of the yacht-filled Portofino harbour was so spectacular it made me want to go there immediately, stay at the Hotel Splendido, live there, die there—even if it did mean dunking my own tea bags.

Although residing at the Hotel Splendido is out of the question—an overnight stay would relieve Geoffrey's wallet of something like a thousand dollars at this time of year, and our beautiful Santa Margherita apartment is close enough for a stay to not be necessary—we can at least go and look at the place and pretend for a few hours that we are part of the hedonistic scene.

We opt to take a boat into Portofino for our first visit, to experience entering the harbour from the water. Like every other day it is gloriously sunny, the sea a blue too perfect to be real. It far surpasses my fantasies as we sail around the corner from Santa Margherita and into the harbour—the hills, the bougainvillea-walled villas, the Hotel Splendido looking proudly out over the water. Portofino really is, as someone once described it, heaven's gift to the postcard industry. Except that there is a decided lack of beautiful people here this day, just overweight tourists like us wearing shabby T-shirts and tatty backpacks. But there is one beautiful couple, who we follow off the boat and check out from behind. She is in a mint green tight-fitting dress, with many strings of pearls around her lovely neck and a pair of very high heels that have her tottering over the cobblestones in the square. She looks lush and lovely but out of place among the T-shirts. He has on a pair of pale lime shorts (I thought Italian men never wore shorts) and a matching jacket slung rakishly over his shoulders. They are too attractive, too well dressed and, although they are the look I expected to see in Portofino, they look wrong somehow.

Portofino seems very small. We take a slow wander around the harbour and slobber outside the windows of shops I wouldn't dare go into—especially the one with nothing in the window apart from a fat round pale pink cushion (a thing we used to call a 'pouf') on which sits a matching pale pink single, perfect Louis Vuitton handbag with a multi-digit price tag. We then walk up the narrow steps, passing heavy ivy-covered gates that offer not even an intriguing peep of the luxurious villas behind them. We come out to a square bit of garden and a church, with a man sitting at the gate asking for money. I object to this because I don't think God would want to charge us to come into one of His houses (and He definitely wouldn't if He is a She), and I certainly wouldn't make Him/Her pay to come into mine—so we wander back down again and do another round of the harbour front. And that is it; Portofino done in an hour. Unless we do lunch.

I want to, but Geoffrey is looking particularly nervous because it is obvious that nothing on any of the menus in the inviting restaurants lining the water's edge is going to be in his stingy price bracket. But this place, this scene, this harbour, these yachts, these hills, these villas, this sun and this water—we may never be here again. Let's splurge.

We choose the restaurant with the prettiest pink tablecloths on small tables closely crammed together right up to the edge of the water. I want a long lunch that stretches on into the hot afternoon after which, feeling full of rich food and boozy bonhomie, I might just remove my outer clothes like the mammas and plunge into the cool waters of the harbour in my corset to entertain the other long-lunching guests.

We order the seafood salad (for me), the gnocchi with pesto (for Geoffrey) and a bottle of chilled white wine (for us both) and sit back to let the afternoon take its course. My seafood salad comes out two minutes later served on a saucer with nothing more than a wedge of lemon; Geoffrey's gnocchi is a similar size, also served on a saucer. These two dishes, while very pleasant—mine has a couple of small squiggly things in it and a heavy mayonnaise, Geoffrey's has that vivid green pesto they make here—take us all of three-and-a-half minutes to eat.

'What are we going to do for the rest of the afternoon?' I ask. It is only just after midday and the restaurant is quickly filling up. I do not want to relinquish our prime table.

'We'll have to order more', Geoffrey says generously, so we call for a salad. Tomato, bocconcini and basil; tiny, on a saucer, once again. We push it around our plates, trying to make it last; we pick up a basil leaf, examine it, put it down again, poke at a chunk of tomato, push it to one side, poke it back to the other, pick up the giant bottle of olive oil left on our table, admire its yellow-green colour, dribble a little onto the salad already doused with too much olive oil and then put our knives and forks down and actually talk to each other. Still we cannot eke out that salad beyond five minutes. Bread. We have some bread to mop up the olive oil. This takes up another seven minutes.

'More wine, we can order more wine', I say, not only because the bottle is empty and we can often be pisspots, but also because this should allow us to hold on to our table for another half-hour at least.

A woman at the next table (just five centimetres away, she could have been part of our fabulous fun) is joined by a stylishly dressed man. He is obviously Italian, she from northern England, judging by her accent. She speaks in a confident nasal voice about her job selling kitchenware. On she goes about the merits of heavy-based saucepans and flat-bottomed frying pans while he nods seriously and tries to comment, but does not have a hope of getting in a single word. The pros and cons of the pressure cooker are analysed in multifarious detail before the advantages of a wok over a steamer are given a thorough going-over. He nods politely, pushes up the sleeves of his Armani jacket and does a good job of looking interested.

Witnessing one of the world's most boring subjects being discussed so earnestly in one of the world's most glorious locations fascinates us for another thirty minutes and takes us to the bottom of our second bottle of wine. When our neighbour turns to the riveting subject of the braising pan versus the electric frypan, we decide it is time to take our leave. Our waiter obviously does too, as there is by now a long line of people after this top table. We pay the enormous bill, me soothing Geoffrey with promises of working until I am ninety-five to help pay for this lunch, and totter tipsily off to hire a small boat from a dark and brooding young man in a hole-in-the-wall hire place next door.

Another bottle of wine to take out on the boat? Geoffrey is, by now, getting into this whole self-indulgent scene. 'Bloody oath', I say and we negotiate the cobblestones carefully to a small wine shop, where a friendly woman is delighted to uncork a bottle of local stuff and supply us with paper cups.

Manoeuvering our small wooden boat out of the harbour between these fabulous yachts with two bottles of wine inside us and an entire waterfront of diners watching is not easy, but we manage it without scratching the paint off anything magnificent. Once outside the harbour, within easy sight of two enormous cruise ships anchored in the bay, we really do take off our clothes and jump into the glorious silky water. Splashing happily (make that drunkenly), with the hot sun overhead and so much affluence around us makes for a remarkable afternoon that, although hazy in parts, will stay in our memories forever.

Lying in bed the next morning with blinding headaches and buckets of regret, we decide to head to Portofino again in the afternoon, this time to walk the four kilometres and experience the Hotel Splendido, just for one … and only one … drink.

'We can re-mortgage the house again', I volunteer as Geoffrey once more peers anxiously into his wallet. 'Just a drink at Splendido, just one', I promise him. I must experience this place. I must.

We walk along the narrow winding road from Santa Margherita to Portofino, looking down the rocky embankment to small strips of beach crowded with people swimming, throwing frisbees and sun-worshiping. We pass tiny coves, old castles, a lovely church, expensive restaurants, wildflowers and roses along the way and, just before Portofino, we take a path that leads up the hill to the Hotel Splendido. The leafy lanes flanked with ivy-covered trees are a fitting and pretty lead-up to the hotel, and we are soon in the bottom of the hotel grounds, where the gardens run down the slopes to the sea. Lavender bushes grow beneath old olive trees, bougainvillea tumbles in trimmed order everywhere and as we climb the path, the gardens become more and more landscaped, and very beautiful.

As people do when they enter a grand hotel where they are not in-house guests, we check our appearance, take on the guilty look of gatecrashers and wonder if a security man will order us out. This uncomfortable feeling intensifies as we enter the car park packed with sporty Porsches, sleek Mercedes and topless Jaguars.

'God I wish I was rich', I tell Geoffrey. 'It's your fault we're not.' He doesn't deign to answer, just leads me up to the terrace, where tables sheltered by protective umbrellas overlook the harbour. Extravagant, padded lounge chairs call out to us, invite us to sit down, but we aren't sure we are allowed to. Out comes an immaculate, bow-tied waiter.

'A drink?' he invites.

'Yes, please.'

'Of course, sit down.'

He makes us feel more than welcome and we sink into the plush seats, order gin-and-tonics, gaze out over the billion-dollar view and slip into fantasy land. My fantasy is, if I may say so, a generous one. It is not the hot one with my suave Italian man. I have another, more family-oriented one ...

I have just won fifty million dollars in the lotto. I charter a private jet to take Geoffrey and our three offspring and their boyfriends/girlfriends to Italy. We drink Krug on the plane and enjoy massages by a bronzed Swedish masseuse we have employed for the trip (okay, too clichéd; let's make him an old Thai man with strong hands and masterful ancient Thai massaging skills). We arrive in Italy refreshed and excited. Several silver stretch limousines take us from Rome to Portofino, where a yacht of ostentatious extravagance awaits us, fully crewed and fully stocked. Its back deck, where we spend most of our time, has a large table where we gather over long meals of every excess. A side table bends under the weight of icy buckets of Bollinger, Louis Roederer and Moët. For one week our family sails the beautiful waters of the Mediterranean, enjoying the indulgences of our combined fantasies and, most importantly—for I am a loving mother—we are all together. And during this week, the gods will have decreed that no matter how much food and wine is consumed, no fat cells will gather on any thigh, buttock or belly. We will then return home and settle down to routines and be the modest, humble people we actually are, lovers of the simple pleasures in life, knowing that we know what it is like to be filthy rich, just for a week.

It is not difficult to get carried away with fantasies while sitting up here on the terrace of the Hotel Splendido, because such ostentatious yachts do exist—they are right down there below us. They do have the back decks with big tables decorated with extravagant displays of flowers. There are people on board who actually live like this. Later, on another trip, another time, we see many of these yachts in Elba and Monaco. We have our photograph taken in front of them like the gawking tourists we are. Many of the yachts have helicopters on the top (I should have included one of those in my fantasy), but a lot also have bored-looking woman sitting on the back decks, watching the pleasures onshore.

Our Hotel Splendido waiter brings our gin-and–tonics, along with small silver dishes of nuts. Everything is placed on the table with elegant little gestures. This is not confined to the Hotel Splendido, for we have noticed this all over Italy. Even in the most humble café, the simplest of dishes is placed before us with as much pride and flourish as if it was a dish of rare and expensive fare. We sip, nibble, sip, nibble, fantasise. This is too gorgeous to leave.

'Let's have another drink', I tell Geoffrey, who adopts that fretful look again. Another round, more dishes of simple nuts served with pride and then a bill for the equivalent of eighty dollars. For four drinks.

We wander down to the harbour, shocked at the cost of this place, and stare at the lucky people rich enough to dine in the cafés and restaurants.

'Lunch yesterday was enough, we can't afford dinner here too', Geoffrey says firmly.

'But we may never be back here again', I nag. We choose Ristorante Delfino, with its merry blue awnings and terracotta tubs of geraniums, right on the waterfront. We eat simply—spaghetti with pesto, bread, one only bottle of wine—and like our lunch yesterday, the meal is over almost before it begins. Thirty (splendid) minutes later and a bill for the equivalent of two hundred and forty dollars and we are on our way, walking back to Santa Margherita with me repeating all the way home that 'we may never be back here again'.

But we do go back again. The following year we find ourselves back on the sunny terrace of the Hotel Splendido, glasses of chilled white wine in our hands and dishes of Ligurian olives by our sides as we look down through the white gardenias and red geraniums to the yachts in the harbour below. This time, one of the yachts actually is ours. Okay, for one hedonistic week only, but it really is ours. All right, along with a hundred other people, but still, it is ours. We are on a Star Clipper cruise of the Mediterranean and I write the following boastful piece in the *Sunshine Coast Daily* when I return home:

If I got up and walked past the Ferraris and Porsches in the car park, down through the leafy pathways adjacent to the hotel, I could see my own fabulous yacht anchored just outside the harbour, waiting for me to finish my late-afternoon dalliance at the Hotel Splendido. On board, my chef will be preparing a multi-course dinner of voluptuous choices and my waiter will be chilling the wine, polishing the glassware and laying out the silverware.

My captain will be on the bridge, studying charts and plotting tomorrow's course through the Mediterranean Sea.

I have sailed into Portofino the day before on this millionaire's yacht, from Monte Carlo, where I had amused myself for an hour in the casino, wandered up to the Grimaldi Palace, checked out the designer-filled boutiques and sat at the Café du Paris sipping a coffee while watching heavily jewelled women walk heavily jewelled poodles up and down the famous footpath.

Tomorrow, after an evening of laid-back entertainment on board, followed by a smooth night's sailing and a sinful breakfast of eggs made to my exact instructions (lightly fried on both sides with a small serving of sautéed mushrooms, thank you), I'll arrive on the island of Elba, where my princess of the sea will anchor beside other lesser yachts and I'll wander through the ancient streets and walk on the tracks of the old Romans, the Medici family and Napoleon, and then I'll board again and take a glass of French bubbles up onto the deck to watch my handsome captain put up the sails and glide me smoothly out of the harbour and into the pink sunset.

God, I sounded like a prat. I was trying to express what it felt like to be on the Star Clipper and live as a fair dinkum rich bitch for a week. The Star Clipper is a replica of the famous clipper sailing ships of the late nineteenth century, but is fitted out as a millionaire's private yacht. It is one of three magnificent clippers in the fleet of the Star Clipper company and is about sailing in the old fashioned way, but with every modern comfort and luxury at your call. No more than one hundred and seventy guests are on board and the attentive and courteous crew of eighty made for a most pleasing ratio.

An oak-panelled library, a piano lounge, a tropical deck bar, a sunbathing deck space and two swimming pools were all I needed in between ports to occupy and entertain me. There were no Las Vegas-style shows on board, no bingo or talent shows, although the crew did put on a delightful amateur show where their vocal talents were almost as good as their seafaring expertise. It is the closest I will ever get to fulfilling my fantasy.

The casino in Monte Carlo appeared much smaller than when I first saw it thirty years earlier, when Geoffrey and I travelled through the south of France on a motorbike. I will never forget the way we zoomed right up to the front of the casino and almost caused the top-hatted, gold-braided doorman to have a seizure and collapse on the footpath. He was busy guiding in sleek Rolls Royces and was so startled to see a couple of big, scruffy Antipodeans pull up outside his hallowed doors on a motorbike, he shouted loudly and angrily at us to leave immediately. This was not an uncommon occurrence back then; distinguished doormen in opulent hotels often told us to scuttle off. We spent the entire summer pressing our noses to hotel and café windows, wondering what it would be like to actually sit down and enjoy a cup of coffee or a meal inside instead of dining by the side of the road or in a dusty camp site. We never once had a meal out anywhere that whole summer of 1970 but hey ... we had a wonderful time and holidayed for four months on a few hundred dollars. So, what am I complaining about? I'll shut up now.

Nine

Some people enjoy travelling in a foreign country without knowing a word of the language. Some—especially Americans, and I hate to stereotype and pick on them because I love Americans very much— expect to be spoken to in English no matter where they go. We see examples of it everywhere; they address shopkeepers, waiters, hotel receptionists and bus drivers in rapid English, confidently assuming they will be understood. Most often they are, because English is becoming more and more prevalent throughout the world, as you well know. But I consider it impolite when in Italy to sit down in a restaurant or board a bus or approach a train station and address someone in English without a polite *'Parla Inglese?'* first. I wouldn't want, or expect, an Italian to come up to me in the street in Australia and start asking directions in their own language. (I also like to understand what people are saying around me ever since seeing that ridiculous scene in *National Lampoon's European Vacation* when waiters in a Parisian restaurant call Chevy Chase a dickhead and all sorts of other obnoxious and insulting things as he smiles and laughs and thinks they are heaping compliments on him.)

So, making the decision to learn Italian two weeks before setting off to Italy was leaving it a bit late, but this is generally the way I go about running my life. It is also why I live in a constant muddle, and probably the main reason I have waited until the very old age of fifty-something to finally write a book.

'It might be helpful when catching trains and buses and things if we spoke a little Italian, don't you think?' I asked Geoffrey a fort-night before we left.

'I'm not going to bother', he answered. 'You do it if you want to.'

So I bought language tapes and a walkman. I walk for an hour every morning in the Noosa National Park and thought it would be the perfect time to do something useful besides walking. Full of determination, I headed off at six every morning with my head-phones on, striding through the park listening to the tapes, repeating the Italian phrases because the voice on the tape told me I must say the words and phrases aloud if I am ever going to get anywhere.

'*Buon giorno*', I called out as I marched along the coastal tracks. This seemed to startle other regular walkers in the park, probably because they are used to seeing me silent and surly every morning, eyes averted, walking with my head down. Although I appear to be a stuck-up bitch, I am not really. I am just shy sometimes, and I also don't like engaging in hearty 'good mornings' all the way through the park with strangers who are probably shy too and also hate forced salutations but feel obliged to participate in them because we are all fellow walkers and it seems the courteous thing to do.

People I have been passing in the park regularly for ten years, who have never had a single 'good morning' out of me, suddenly found themselves confronted with a booming *'buon giorno'* and were, understandably, a bit surprised. A few of them actually said it back, but mostly they looked at me as though I was deranged.

'Quanta costa il biglietto per Napoli?' I continued. *'A che ora arriva il treno da Roma?'*

What is the fare to Naples? When does the train from Rome arrive? These were obviously going to be useful questions to ask in Italy, but there was not much call for them in the Noosa National Park. The odd looks from other walkers started to embarrass me, so I took to the privacy of the inland tracks where very few walkers go.

Every morning for two weeks I wore my headphones while walking deep into the quiet rainforest peace of the Tanglewood track. The Tanglewood track is an 8.4 kilometre round trip of isolated inland track. It meanders through eucalyptus wetlands, closed woodlands and thrilling rainforest. The first section, through tall green ferns beneath a canopy of lofty trees, is so lovely and quiet I could not bear to speak my Italian words aloud. On sunny mornings, shafts of early sunlight, as thin as straw in some places, as thick as telephone poles in others, filtered through the trees. The sounds of the awakening rainforest—the call of birds, the cackle of kookaburras, the scratching of bush turkeys, the fait whoosh of the distant ocean—were too thrilling, too precious to be drowned out by an Italian voice telling me how to ask a taxi driver to take me to the airport in Milan. A few steps into the Tanglewood track each morning I had to pull off the headphones and walk along freely, inhaling the dewy rainforest smell, listening to the birds calling to each other, looking out for goannas, koalas and bush turkeys.

Suffice to say, my Noosa National Park Italian lessons did not go well. I could not concentrate on the tapes while surrounded by so much of nature's beauty, so on our return from Italy in 2000,

I did what I should have done years ago—I enrolled in Italian-language classes.

About fifteen of us turned up for the Saturday morning beginners' class. Francesca, our dark, attractive teacher who comes from northern Italy, began by taking us through the Italian alphabet, making us sound out the letters aloud. We discovered that *ch* is a hard sound like a *k*, and that when a *c* is followed by an *i* or *e*, it takes on a *ch* sound. When *gl* is followed by *i*, the sound is similar to the *lli* in *million*. And so on as the list continued.

We were all appalling students. Our accents sounded twangy, grating, ghastly, and we could not get used to a *c* (followed by an *e* or *i*) having a *ch* sound, so kept pronouncing *cinque* (five) as *sinque*. For years I had been pronouncing *pancetta* as *pansetta* and *porcini* as *porseeni* (and you will agree that, seeing as I am a food writer, this was a serious mistake indeed). Now, almost a year since that first Italian lesson and having finally grasped the whole *ci* and *ce* thing, I cannot abide people—mostly chefs and restaurant waiting staff—pronouncing Italian words incorrectly.

'Our Caesar salad has pansetta in it, not bacon', some poor waiter might say to me, and I would practically leap out of my seat and hit him.

'Panchetta. It is pronounced *panchetta*.'

'Yeah, that's what I said: *pansetta*.'

'No, no. *Ch, ch, ch*', I would then say. 'It has a *ch* sound as in *church*.'

'Yeah, *pansetta*', he would retort, looking at me as though he wanted to whack me over the head with his big fat phallic pepper grinder. And if I keep on correcting waiters on their pronunciation, one day I will be hit over the head with a pepper grinder, and deserve it.

Anyway, after that first scary Italian class, only about half of the fifteen came back for a second attempt. The third week, after I had become totally confused by the different endings for feminine and masculine nouns (and wondered why a saucepan should be a woman and a hat should be a man), only six of us came back. We were all woeful and our Italian accents had not improved; if anything, they had become worse. Whenever Francesca read aloud in Italian to us the language sounded outrageously romantic, as sexy as hell and perfectly attuned to her graceful appearance (and I am certain it made the two men in the class have unwholesome thoughts about her), but when we repeated the same piece out loud it stank.

After the first month our numbers dwindled even further and we were reduced to myself and three other women about my age who studied hard and did their homework but still struggled. To make matters worse, I often arrived still groggy from a big Friday night dinner party, scruffy and T-shirted, causing Francesca—a woman in full possession of *bella figura*, that indefinable something Italians have that makes them look perpetually confident and beautiful and that no Australian could ever hope to achieve—to have a mild attack of the vapours.

Francesca must have thought her little class of Aussies was made up of a bunch of ignorant dags, the possessors of *brutta figura*, which I think translated has something to do with uncouth yobbos. A year later, I was still hopeless at Italian, bottom of the class and convinced the only way I would ever truly grasp the language would be to go and live in Italy for at least a year, possibly two or even five. I'm working on that.

Attending classes with middle-aged students seeking a new learning experience can be an entertaining as well as enlightening experience. I had not inquired of my fellow Italian-language students why they wanted to speak Italian because, quite frankly, just like me, not one of them appeared to have even the remotest possibility of making themselves understood if they ever got to Italy.

Australia is probably full of classes of mature-aged students learning something new right now—hopeful old people going through mid-life crises thinking their lives will change for the better because they are learning something.

About ten years ago I attended college with a group of middle-aged would-be novelists and, although not one of us could write a well-constructed sentence, let alone a good short story and God forbid an intelligent novel, it was an experience in the study of human nature the likes of which I have not come across since.

We had a nun in the class; I forget her name, but she was sweet, so I'll call her Sister Sweetie. We also had a former prostitute from Germany who was cynical and opinionated and I forget her name too so I'll call her Helga, because that's the only German name I can think of. We had to workshop our work, read aloud what we had written and then critique each other's work.

The nun wrote a children's story in which tall friendly trees reached their verdant branches up to the sun and smiled lovingly down on babbling brooks and dancing fairies. The prostitute wrote an autobiography of her awful life as an ageing hooker.

Sister Sweetie would read aloud several paragraphs of her work where fairies and little furry creatures played happily in a sylvan glade while the grand old tree smiled benignly at them and the brook babbled with joy. We would all sit and listen with benign expressions, swept away for a brief time on a babbling brook of innocence. Then we would cross to Helga, whose first paragraph read something like, 'I hate men; I have fucked thousands of them; they all have dirty bums. I'd much rather pull down my pants, spread my legs and pleasure myself'.

Needless to say, we would go from feeling warm and fuzzy to being horrified and disgusted in the course of ten minutes. It was extraordinary, but definitely a learning experience because I never knew all men had dirty bums, did you?

Our tutor took it all in—goodness knows what she must have thought of us—and attempted to teach us about the mechanics of good writing, how to construct plots, how to write popular fiction and how to write good romance novels and make a small fortune. (As far as I know, no-one from the class ever did.)

'You must use euphemisms if you want to write Mills and Boon stories', she said. 'You must be careful when writing love scenes; keep them romantic rather than sexy.' She was a very good teacher when she became involved like this, and quite outstanding when she became animated.

'Do not give me explicit terms for body parts', she said forcefully one day, giving Helga a meaningful look. 'And stay above the waist; that is acceptable. Nothing below the waist, please. Nipples are okay, but they should be in, not out. And always give me trembling thighs and flaring nostrils.'

By this stage, all the old men in the class had begun breathing heavily. It was difficult not to laugh out loud, especially when the tutor suddenly thumped the desk vigorously and commanded, 'Never give me a hard penis; always give me a throbbing member'.

While the Italian language is lovely to learn, I found out on later trips to Italy that having a little Italian in your vocabulary can sometimes be more of a hindrance than a help. Approaching a ticket seller at a station and being able to say '*Due biglietti per Roma, per favore*' (two tickets for Rome, please), while being pretty bloody impressive, is actually no good at all. The ticket seller will assume you speak Italian and fire back rapid sentences at you, going faster and faster as he asks, 'First or second class? Express or stopping at all stations? With or without a buffet carriage?', to which you nod agreement because you are delighted to have impressed him with your Italian in the first place and do not want him to know you are really an ignorant fraud and have not understood a word he has just said. He will then issue you with an expensive first-class ticket with full buffet carriage privileges you didn't want, and then go on to speak rapidly in Italian again: 'Your train will leave from platform seven, but that could change so listen for the announcements and you do know, don't you, that you may have to change stations at Milan and then go over to platform thirteen, but that might also change, so make sure you ask the inspector on board and he will direct you on your arrival in Milan, and have a lovely day, and I must say you are a hot-looking woman and I really admire your titties', and off you go happily unenlightened, without having understood a single word he said, and get on the wrong train and arrive in Florence at dinner time, having missed your lunchtime appointment in Rome.

It is all very confusing, and made worse when you think about it because it is almost a certainty that the ticket seller spoke English and could have told you all this important information (especially the bit about your nice titties) in your own tongue, had you approached him in it in the first place—with a polite '*Parla Inglese?*' first, of course.

Ten

Food and Italy. The two words are synonymous and I'm going to be talking quite a bit about food in this chapter, but I'll try not to get carried away with gustatory prose. I want to share with you some glorious meals Geoffrey and I enjoyed from one end of Italy to another. I'll also let you in on the details of some that were not so glorious but memorable anyway for the extraordinary settings in which they were served.

In our beloved Santa Margherita (yes, we are still in this gorgeous place, but we'll move on soon), we search on and on for our mamma in a rustic *ristorante*. Our delight in Italian eateries is unending, but we begin to tire of the same pizzas, spaghetti and *antipasti* in all the tourist restaurants.

Italy's joy at the table is evident everywhere, but we seem unable to discover the passion for food preparation, the pleasure in offering good fresh produce. We begin to wonder if it is only in the home kitchen (and on Antonio Carluccio's television program) that meals are prepared with love and flourish. We have known Italian food in Australia to be brave and daring, often taking modern twists on old favourites. In Melbourne's Lygon Street we have eaten veal covered with thick, rich tomato sauce and melting mozzarella that was so good it rendered us temporarily speechless. We have plunged our forks into mountainous dishes of steaming spaghetti sticky with cream, bacon and parmesan. We have sat in suburban Italian cafés all over Melbourne and feasted on meaty lasagnas, linguini brimming with fat mussels, gnocchi in sensuous gorgonzola sauces, and tiramisu rich with mascarpone beneath layers of cream and shaved chocolate.

We have not tasted this kind of Italian food in Italy yet, but are not disappointed; the unique ambience in even the most humble of Italy's restaurants more than satisfies.

Curious to know what the 'rich' salad is in one small Santa Margherita *ristorante*, we order it with expectations of vine-ripened tomatoes and freshly plucked basil drizzled with local extra virgin olive oil. A short while later we receive a plate of canned tuna, frozen peas and corn, plain black olives, a dried-up artichoke and half of a very hard boiled egg.

In Siena (more about this glorious place later) we sit in the magnificent Piazza del Campo agog at the beauty of the ancient buildings in the famous square and, in this most spectacular of settings, eat the most unspectacular of food. Our bow-tied waiter guides us through the menu. His strong recommendation is the *antipasti* to start, followed by the chef's specialty of *parmigiana di melanzane* (eggplant with parmesan). It sounds wonderful; it is not. What we receive, with the customary flourish and pride, is a small plate on which sit three slices of re-heated fried eggplant, two strips of re-heated fried zucchini and a raw tomato cut in half. The chef's specialty doesn't fare any better: three slices of the same tired eggplant layered with canned tomato purée and sprinkled meanly with packaged parmesan. It is quite awful, but we should have expected it—any restaurateur fortunate enough to own a restaurant in such a compelling setting can get away with anything.

This poor meal is, of course, our own fault. There are many good meals to be experienced in tourist spots and we should have done more research before leaving Australia.

We do, however, find an exceptional *ristorante* right below our Santa Margherita apartment. A foodie friend recommended it before we left. 'It's very good', she said. 'Not cheap, about a hundred dollars a head, no menu, the food just keeps on coming out.'

When we telephone to make a reservation, we hear the owner's voice not only on the end of the phone, but also down below us in the street. We are sitting on top of our friend's recommendation and have passed it every day without noticing, probably because of its unpretentious frontage. We have not even noticed its name, although we have heard lively clatter and smelt garlicky, fishy aromas wafting up every evening. So down we go to Trattoria Cesarina, full of anticipation.

We receive a loud and warm Italian greeting from the owner and his (obvious) line-up of family members. A glass of chilled white fizz is poured and a small plate of fresh figs and thin slices of salami is whizzed out to us. This is a very good start.

We sip, munch and look around. The interior of the restaurant is long and slim and very pretty, with pink tablecloths, big vases of fresh flowers and bathtub-sized bowls filled with bottles of local wine. On wooden tables down the centre of the restaurant sit fat bottles of olive oil and deep bowls filled with giant dried mushrooms.

We relax and let it happen. Course after course comes out of the kitchen, each to first sit on the centre wooden tables, where our waiter douses it liberally with olive oil before tossing, swirling or cutting, depending on what it is, and portioning it out on white plates. Only then is the finished dish swung theatrically through the air and placed gently before us.

All around us the tables fill with big family crowds. The noise level rises and the atmosphere is everything we have hoped to experience in Italy. We eat fresh butterflied anchovies, deep fried and served with stuffed zucchini flowers. Next, mussels and unknown local shellfish tossed through tagliatelle. Then, polenta and pancetta, seafood salad full of little blobs of fresh octopus, a frittata studded with yet more seafood, grilled fish with those pungent porcini, all washed down with a bottle of light red barolo wine. We finish with chunks of hard tasty cheese, fresh walnuts we crack ourselves and delicate petits fours with strong coffee. All around us, everyone is served the same number of courses. The waiters rush in and out of the kitchen and every time a dish comes out, the huge bottles of olive oil are lifted high into the air to let a small river of golden oil stream enticingly down onto the food. The large amount of oil shocks us, but confirms our opinion that no serious food-loving Italian would dream of eating anything unless it is drowning in this life-preserving oil.

We have a magical evening of food, wine, culinary theatre and intriguing people. It is a meal voluptuous in its number of courses and well worth the two hundred and fifty dollar bill and Geoffrey's corresponding anxiety.

Another memorable meal (for different reasons) takes place in a particularly narrow backstreet in Vernazza in the Cinque Terre. I love the atmosphere of these constricted streets; the

tall, multicoloured buildings forming a shady chasm on the cobbled street, the omnipresent washing flapping on lines from every
apartment, the tiny souvenir shops set into attractive little holes
in the walls, kids kicking a football among the inevitable stream
of tourists, restaurants that consist of no more than a tiny kitchen
on one side of the street and a little temporarily erected wooden
platform holding tables on the other.

It is at such a place we decide to eat. The wooden platform is
so small and the tables for two are so crammed together, they
actually look like one long table for eight. As we pull up a table
for two, we're unable to avoid disturbing the other diners on
the platform, because no-one can get in or out without making
everyone else stand up, move bums and belongings, then sit down
again, all the while ducking to avoid the washing that flaps
overhead.

We sit next to a man dining alone, and next to him are a couple of blokes. The only table vacant—the one to our right—soon
fills with a young German couple. When they arrive, everyone
stands, shuffles and sucks in bellies as the Germans pick their
way over and around us to the last table. The platform is now full.
The closeness of the tables—they are just two tiny centimetres
apart—creates a dilemma: it is as though we are at one long
table, and thus feel obliged to make conversation with our fellow
diners. But those two centimetres make a big difference; they
separate us and create perimeters around our tables for two,
making us independent couples (apart from the single man) with
no obligation to speak to each other. We have separate tablecloths, a tiny vase of flowers each, a candle for two. I am overcome
with self-consciousness. To speak or not to speak? The closeness
makes me claustrophobic.

Geoffrey looks stupidly at me and I look stupidly at him. We are too ill at ease to talk to each other, nervous our conversation will appear foolish to the others, as it normally does to us. Everyone else in our row appears to feel the same way, because conversation dries up. The waiter runs the three steps across from the kitchen on the other side of the road to deliver bread and water, so once again everyone stands, shuffles and sucks in stomachs to let him pass. I want to leap up and run out screaming with suffocation and embarrassment. But to do that would mean everyone standing up again, unless I am prepared to climb out over the tables. I take deep breaths, relax, order spaghetti with tomato sauce then a pizza, and lower my head to avoid looking at anyone. The man next to us has a plate of pasta with those prawns that have big heads that come off to leave you with a minuscule bit of flesh. Fortunately, the dismantling of the prawn heads occupies him and he focuses on his plate. The couple on our right starts to converse in German, which relaxes me. The two blokes on the end concentrate on the flapping washing.

Our food comes and everyone stands for the shuffling routine, which we have all mastered by now. The food is excellent. We expected ordinariness in a place so tiny, but the spaghetti is perfect; generous, hot and full of bits of flavoursome red tomatoes. Our pizza is also good; thin-crusted with plenty of stringy mozzarella. We want to linger over our food and enjoy it, but I cannot. I give Geoffrey big eye-rolling looks every time he speaks, because I fear our conversation is so dull that everyone who has been privy to it— and that is everyone on the platform—will laugh out loud at these two boring old Aussies. (You will have gathered that it does not take much for me to become self-conscious: greeting people in the Noosa National Park, a close encounter with a neighbouring table in a small restaurant ... I need therapy.)

Eventually, our man with the big prawn heads finishes his meal and reaches for something under the table; suddenly a dog almost as big as him puts its big woolly head out and startles everyone on the platform. The man and his dog are ready to leave and this means an entire evacuation of the platform, mainly because the huge dog, released from its under-the-table prison, is ready to frolic. It gambols clumsily between diners, sniffs at tables and looks in dire need of a pee. I have to leave, even though the food is fantastic and unfinished. I race the few steps across the road to the souvenir shop and browse while Geoffrey pays the bill and everyone on the platform returns to their meals.

I once interviewed the chef/owner of one of Queensland's busiest and most successful Italian restaurants. He had just won a national competition for making the best pizzas in Australia. In the competition, he had to make four pizzas—a meat, a seafood, a vegetarian and a specialty version—in front of discerning judges and a crowd of people at a cook-off in Melbourne.

This man had gone to breathtaking gustatory lengths with his toppings. His meat pizza was layered with cranberry sauce and topped with turkey, walnuts, asparagus, fetta and so many other ingredients I've forgotten them now. His seafood pizza was piled with prawns, scallops, red pepper and caramelised onions. The vegetarian version was awash with chargrilled sweet potato, pumpkin, broccoli and mushrooms on a sweet potato purée. His specialty—a colourful concoction with brown sugar and cinnamon folded through the base—was patterned prettily with caramelised bananas, macadamia nuts, berry coulis-stuffed profiteroles topped with rich dark-chocolate sauce, and finished off with cream and ice-cream in the middle.

'What do you think Italians would think of all this stuff on top of a pizza?' I asked the chef.

'Don't know', he replied.

'Do you think we have taken the pizza too far, done too much with it?' I asked.

'No, not at all.'

'But a pizza is meant to be tomato, mozzarella, maybe anchovies. What do you think about Australian chefs putting a Thai chicken curry on top of a pizza?' I continued.

'It's our most popular one', he said.

Romance is easy to find in many restaurants in Italy. Ambience, I mean; you and your partner must provide the romance, but there are a number of places so heartbreakingly romantic, even the most hard-hearted would succumb. And yes, I'm going to tell you about them.

La Stalla, high on the hill above Santa Margherita and overlooking the bay, is one of the most romantic restaurants of them all. Our taxi driver tells us so as he drives us up the hill.

'*Molto romantico*', he says and kisses his fingers. We already know this because we have passed it during one of our late-afternoon treks. We have wandered up the long driveway to La Stalla (*stalla* apparently means stables, so we presume the restaurant was stables in a former life) and seen the tables set with pale pink cloths and fresh flowers, gleaming glasses and sparkling cutlery. We have noted the candles inside small glass holders, spotted the dishes of cherry tomatoes on all the tables and gasped over the racks of old and vintage wines.

We have made a reservation for Sunday evening, but turn up to find our name not on the list. 'But we definitely booked', we tell the owner, a charming and good-looking man. *'No problema'*, he says and gives us the best table, right by the window. Another is set up at the back for the people who, we soon discover, we have cheated out of this prime position. In our holiday stupor we have turned up on the wrong night. It is Saturday and the restaurant is fully booked, but our debonair host discreetly declines to mention our mistake and we love him for it (and it's one of the reasons he's getting a big plug here).

Everything about La Stalla is of the highest standard. On each table, little dishes of intriguing *antipasti* await—plump borlotti beans with prawns, stuffed zucchini flowers, fried anchovies, a ratatouille-style mix of garlicky vegetables and, of course, the good olive oil to splash over it all.

While the food is superb, it is outshone by the views down to the harbour and across to the distant hills. The view changes over the long evening, from deep green, soft red and vivid blue to pale purple and delicate mauve and then to starry wonder as thousands of lights in homes and villas are switched on to create a twinkling fairyland before us.

There are many choices after the *antipasti*, including pastas to be taken as *secondo piatto*, then meat or fish followed by dessert, then cheese and fruit. Geoffrey and I order a mushroom risotto to share and happily wait half an hour for it, assured it is being freshly cooked to order. We cast guilty glances to the table at the back, to the people we have usurped from this prime seat at the front. Our glasses are filled and refilled before our risotto is brought out, wheeled to our table in a polished copper saucepan sitting on a small trolley and served out in big bowls. Rich, creamy, hot and perfectly cooked, it is a highlight of our evening and so good it takes our attention away from the view for half an hour.

Ristorante Terrazza Brunella in the Villa Brunella on Capri is another place to sweep you away on a magic carpet of romance. It is likely that many people never even notice the food here, the views are so sexy, so dreamy. A small vase with a single red rose sits on each pink-clothed table, glasses and cutlery gleam and gorgeous waiters glide discreetly past tables. We are given one of the best tables, by the big open windows. The restaurant is high on a cliff, jutting out over the edge so we feel we are suspended in a starry piece of paradise high in the sky. It looks down to the sea and across to towering cliffs that rise grandly from the water and are dotted with villas and small hotels among lush green foliage. We arrive in daylight—the only way one should arrive during the long summer evenings—and sit and watch the changing scene as the soft, slow twilight paints the sky, hills, cliffs and sea with delicate pink, pale green and deep blue. As the evening dawdles its way into night, lights begin to twinkle from the yachts below to be mirrored by the stars high in the sky. Countless marriage proposals must have been made in this restaurant and nights of hot hotel-room passion must have followed many a dinner here, but I'm not going to tell you what Geoffrey and I got up to after our dinner at Ristorante Terrazza Brunella—not because I'm modest, but because I don't want to make you sick.

We are starting to worry about our heavy consumption of olive oil. We use it sparingly at home in Australia—a spray in the wok, a brush on steaks, a drizzle in salsas—but here in Italy we are pouring it with abandon on almost everything. We have gone through two 1-litre bottles in a week at the Santa Margherita apartment. Every time I cut up a tomato, Geoffrey gets a gleam in his eye and reaches for the bottle; I can't eat a slice of bread anymore unless it is soaked in golden oil. We douse our spaghetti with it, pour it on top of pizzas and drown our salads in it. In cafés we become agitated if the bottle of olive oil is not brought to our table the moment we sit down, and we then swirl it over our chicken and trickle it on our fish. We feel like Antonio Carluccio, always reaching for the 'good olive oil'.

We know olive oil is good for us—Hippocrates said so thousands of years ago and doctors tell us it lowers cholesterol and even helps treat high blood pressure—but in terms of weight gain, it is every bit as deadly as butter.

I can't recall ever using olive oil when I was a young, smitten housewife in Southampton in the seventies, desperately trying to impress a new husband. It was all about lard back then. Big fat white blobs of pure lard went into my frying pan for those lovely Sunday morning fry-ups and into my chip pan every night. And lovely it was, too, despite the price I'm paying now of big fat white blobs of lard around my hips.

Even though Australians planted olive trees in the nineteenth century, olive oil was really only introduced to us in a big way in 1956, when the chefs looking after the Italian Olympic team brought crateloads of it with them to Melbourne. Most people in Australia were horrified by this foreign product at first and proceeded to insult the Italian chefs and proudly erect large banners advertising artery-clogging Noon's pies around the perimeter of the Olympic stadium. But some of those Italian chefs stayed on in Australia, opened restaurants, showed us the benefits of the good olive oil and convinced us that there was an alternative to butter or dripping for our bread. Now most pantries in Australia are not complete without a bottle of the stuff. In fact, Australia now has its own flourishing olive oil industry.

I imagine the Italians would be proud not only of Australia's ability to produce spectacular olive oil, but also of our skill in making Limoncello, the heady lemon drink they love, especially in the south. Originating on the Amalfi coast, Limoncello is like sunshine in a glass, with an agreeable alcoholic kick.

I once interviewed an Italian-born Adelaide restaurateur, Libero De Luca, who began making his own Limoncello in Australia after visiting his homeland and spending time on the Amalfi coast.

'There you see it in every shop, every home, every café', he told me on a visit to Noosa, where he obligingly brought a caseload of Limoncello to our interview. 'You automatically receive it after any meal and even in the barber shop they give you a Limoncello.'

This delicious drink is made with lemons from a centuries-old formula, usually in the Italian home for family consumption. Its fresh citrus fragrance, fresh taste and alcoholic content make it the ideal aperitif with a splash of soda, or a digestive at the end of a meal with nothing more than ice.

De Luca, who has lived in Adelaide for forty-six years and owned four restaurants, spent some time working without pay in a Limoncello factory in Amalfi, where he observed, studied and wrangled secrets from locals before returning to Adelaide to set up his own factory. He says his Limoncello is better than the Italian version because of the superior quality of our Australian lemons.

Each week, about 400 kilograms of lemons arrive at his factory the day after they are picked in the Riverland in South Australia.

Every lemon is zested by hand to ensure no bitter particle is included in the resulting lemon oil. The lemon zest is infused in pure grape alcohol before a syrup of the best spring water and sugar is added. This results in a gorgeous nectar-like sweet, sharp, lemony liqueur.

'In Italy, Limoncello is more popular than Vermouth or Sambuca', he said. 'Business is growing, it's going very well. I even have Italians who buy my Limoncello to take back to Italy.'

De Luca first came to Australia from Naples in 1955 as a nineteen-year-old and settled in Adelaide because he had an uncle there. He left behind a mother who 'is crying all the time' (as you can well imagine) and opened the first pizza bar in South Australia. He then opened a wine bar with the incongruous name of Billy Bunter and began educating Australians in the merits of Italian food, especially the delights of calamari.

'They used to use it as bait', he said. 'I started giving it to them deep fried for free and it took six months but I educated them to it and then I put it on the menu.'

De Luca now employs a small army of staff to keep up with the demand for Limoncello, and has just started manufacturing Chocolatina, an orange-and-chocolate drink that tastes like an alcoholic Jaffa—that just goes to prove that an Italian icon really can be fused with an Aussie one. And I'll drink to that.

Eleven

On my return from Italy I wrote a silly article for my newspaper on the hazards of driving on Italian roads. It was a touch melodramatic and full of artistic licence (massive exaggerations), and some smarty sub-editor gave it the heading, 'The Italian Job—On Driving Mrs Rickard'.

I suppose I am like an old Miss Daisy being driven all over the place, giving spirited back-seat instructions and bossy directions, tut-tutting at every wrong turn, letting out alarming gasps every time another car comes within 500 metres of us, clutching tightly onto the door handle as we drive through a tunnel, grabbing hold of the steering wheel if I think we are going the wrong way around roundabouts. But, if you'll forgive me for saying so, you would too if you were my age and were enduring your first experience on the Formula One racing circuits that masquerade as Italian roads.

We really did leave the hire car parked in the Santa Margherita streets under a growing pile of pigeon poop. We did not use it once. However, we did eventually have to burrow beneath the birdshit—well, Geoffrey did—to get it out to drive it down to Sorrento, where we had planned to drop it off. After a night's stay there, we were heading over to Capri for several weeks of unbridled luxury.

The hire car actually came out of its space without problem, mainly because I wasn't there to interfere. I cowered inside the apartment until Geoffrey got it out, cleaned it and had it ready, waiting and spotless to zip us down the autostrada to Sorrento.

Like most Australians who undertake a car trip—and let's face it, it is always a bloody long trip—we like to leave before dawn to get a few hundred kilometres behind us before the day starts. The drive from northern Italy to southern Italy along the super-efficient autostradas only takes about five hours, a mere trifle for those of us used to driving twice that distance before lunchtime. Once we get out onto the autostrada, free from the succession of long dark tunnels, it isn't too bad at all.

We drive towards Florence, then take the autostrada towards Rome. As the hours and kilometres pass, our confidence grows, as does our fondness for one of the few pleasant things about driving in Italy: the road stops. We began to look forward to these.

At home in Australia we would stop at a petrol station only when we absolutely had to. We could fill up the car and empty our bladders almost at the same time and order the kids back into the car the second they had stretched their legs, all so we could get on our way again. But the Italians take their road comfort seriously. Not for them the quick dash inside for a Styrofoam cup of murky coffee and a greasy sausage roll to take back to the car for messy one-handed consumption along the highway; they make a festive outing of stopping at the Autogrills. I begin to love the Autogrills.

Autogrills are seriously huge and always bustling with activity. Most stretch from one side of the multi-laned autostrada to the other, joined by massive overhead walkways. The Autogrill sells petrol, of course, but is actually an interesting mix of lively super-market, suburban restaurant, frantic newsagent, browsy bookstore, energetic toyshop and well-stocked wine bar.

For the Italians, the Autogrill is a place of friendly welcome, somewhere to water the dog and not only have a good leg stretch, but to make new friends. We love them most of all for their life-giving espressos. An espresso taken at the bar, standing up Italian-style, can give a weary motorist another five hours of energy. These tiny black coffees (about three teaspoons-full) look harmless enough, but are fiendishly strong and give such a quick caffeine hit that we always head back to the car feeling like Michael Schumacher.

It took us many attempts to actually figure out how to purchase the rejuvenating espressos. We eventually realised that coffee and food are only dispensed once a ticket is purchased from a harried person at a hectic cash register in the middle of the crowded Autogrill. Nothing is forthcoming without a ticket.

If one is prone to pinching stuff, this system can be very pro-ductive, not for the coffees, which are served individually from a hissing machine, but for the delicious Italian pastries that sit on the counter in big open jars for honest ticket-buyers to help themselves to. At one stop these pastries prove too tempting for a group of strapping young men carrying backpacks the size of small hotels. These men, with their one ticket each, come back and back, then back and back again to dip their big hands into the pastry jar. No-one but us takes the slightest notice; Italians at roadside stops are far too busy talking about the important things in life such as football and children to care about a bit of pastry pilfering.

I too was tempted to pinch an extra pastry, but everyone knows that when a normally law-abiding middle-aged woman steps out of character, even for one minute, God will punish her big-time. I suspect I am the only guest in the world who does not take the little shampoo bottles, soaps, toothpaste, sewing kits, shower caps, bathrobes, slippers and boot polish paraphernalia from hotel rooms. I once stayed at the wonderfully opulent Palazzo Versace on the Gold Coast in Queensland (where a flimsy little chiffony dress in the lobby shop cost more than my car) and was so paranoid about not pinching anything—especially the elaborate red-and-gold coffee cups resting on top of the mini bar— I left behind the divine little bottles of Versace perfume and bath gel sitting on the marble wash basin next to the gold taps, only to find out later that they were complimentary and meant to be taken.

But, back to Italy. Small teams of chefs in Autogrills cook non-stop, and the variety and amount of food keeps me interested for weeks. We can have freshly baked woodfired pizzas, fat focaccias, *panini*, the full *antipasti* works or a spaghetti meal, or perhaps some suckling pig if we feel the urge. It's quite marvellous.

In the supermarket section, everything we could possibly want is there, from giant bottles of olive oil and Belgian chocolates to canned tomatoes and fresh fruit and vegetables. The choices are dazzling. I could easily do all my Christmas shopping under this roof. Toys, games, books, gifts; everything for the entire family is here. I bet if I asked I could have had a hair cut and colour here too, or perhaps a leg wax or even a facial. At every Autogrill stop we get so carried away by the variety of goods available, by the convenience, the comfort, the jovial nature of it all, we come out carrying big packages of groceries, fruit, chocolates—a beach ball once—deli products and dozens of bottles of wine. Sometimes we even buy petrol.

We drive easily down the length of Italy, growing cockier as each kilometre slips away. The countryside changes as we drive further south, leaving behind the fields of waving yellow sunflowers and moving on to factories and industry. We approach Naples pleased we are giving it a wide berth and staying on the autostrada. It is a pity that this big city has such a bad reputation, which leads most tourists to avoid it. Those fearless travellers who ignore stories of pickpockets and handbag snatchers come home raving about Naples, of the discoveries in the backstreets, the unfor-gettable meal in a smoky café, the bargain shopping—and jolly good luck to them, too, but today we do not have the slightest desire to go anywhere near Naples. I remember stepping off the Italian ship at Naples all those years ago, giddy with sexual power and swept away by the European-ness of it. But now, looking out the car window, all I can say is that I am glad the autostrada skirts around Naples.

We approach the tollbooths near Naples at crawling pace, the traffic horrendously built up, our good mood evaporating. After we pay and inch through the booths, we come out on the other side into what seems like a truck drivers' strike. Possibly every enormous truck and lorry in Italy has gathered and stopped on the wide highway in one jangled mess. Trucks point every way; backwards, forwards, some sideways across three lanes, others with noses touching, yet more with backs touching. I have never seen so many trucks on a road, let alone stopped in such a tangled, clogged mess. We are right in the middle of it and, by the look of the gridlock, there will be no going forward or backward for at least a month. The truck drivers are all out of their trucks, sitting on any bit of available space on the road, playing cards, shouting, gesticulating and pouring their hearts out in the usual manner of Italians, whether heartbroken or happy.

Cars inch through the eight tollbooths behind us, locking us irrevocably into the messy jam. I roll down the window and ask several men what is happening, but no-one has any English for me today, or at least is not about to let on to a big, pushy Aussie sheila if he does. We sit blocked, trapped, angry, with no clue what is happening and no idea how long we will be here. Our confidence has gone, our strange new feelings of enjoyment of Italian roads have vanished.

'We have the wine', I say after several frustrating hours have passed. 'Let's open one of the bottles and get smashed.'

But Geoffrey, ever optimistic, does not think this a good idea, just in case the traffic starts moving again. More questions out of the window prove fruitless, so we get out and join some of the card players, listening to the angry voices all around. No-one can, or will, give us any information. Several hours, many card games and a few feisty fistfights later (mine and Geoffrey's), some of the men jump up into the cabins of their trucks and begin frantically tooting their horns. Others follow. Soon, every driver is back in his truck with his hand on the horn. The noise is deafening, but at least something is happening. Then, without explanation, the trucks slowly start to move. Centimetre by centimetre they untangle and, with a lot of hand thumping on side doors, horn blowing and shouts of *porca Madonna!*, the jigsaw of trucks begins to unravel.

We slowly move off with the masses, me screaming out the window to truck drivers, 'Scratch this car and you're dead!', because the snooty girl at the hire company has told us that we will have to pay millions of lire for any damage (and several billion if the car is stolen, which is highly likely if we go anywhere near Napoli—her words).

'Watch out! Don't touch us! Get away!', I rant and shout, but no-one takes any notice and it is only Geoffrey's heroic efforts and superior driving ability (this is not quite how I phrase it at the time) that allow us to escape—another hour later—from the awful traffic jam. We never did find out what it was all about. We watched the local news that night, but no sign of the truck gridlock came on. It could have been something as big as a national stop-work meeting of all the unions in Italy, or maybe the truck drivers just wanted a card game. Who knows? It's Italy.

When we visit Italy a year later, I have the responsibility for driving. I can't remember the reason now, but the hire car is in my name and I am the one *and only* person permitted to drive it.

In the twelve months that have passed since our last Italian driving experience we have completely lost confidence again. So would you, don't scoff.

It is really not a good idea to drive in Italy, even if you are young, confident and assured of your linguistic skills (for the all-important asking of directions). But when you are middle-aged (or is that old?), nervous, frightened of speed and have discovered that what you thought was your fantastic grip on the Italian language is, in reality, nothing more than one big linguistic fog, it is pure madness.

But we are committed to the hire car and have to get from Rome to various parts of Tuscany and then to the Ligurian coast. We set off from Rome airport in a nifty little car, jumping and jerking along the road with front and back windscreen wipers flapping happily and windows randomly opening and shutting as we struggle with unfamiliar buttons and blinkers and gearsticks. Out of the city and onto the autostrada, looking forward to an invigorating espresso and a bit of shopping at the Autogrill, we see small cars and huge trucks thunder past us at 140 kilometres per hour while we bump along with wipers waving, windows moving and us cursing the Madonna just like the Italians at a very non-Italian 60 kilometres per hour.

Fifteen minutes later, we start to get the hang of it. We fight and beat the recalcitrant wipers, clam down the frisky windows, conquer the marauding gearstick, and build up enough confidence to take a quick sideways glance towards the unending fields of dancing flowers. Then, just as we are beginning to enjoy the day, we come across our first tollbooth; a very automatic tollbooth; with no-one helpful manning it. These monsters appear all too frequently and require money to be paid (fair enough) but often have no-one within sight to help morons such as us.

Like anything, once you know how things work, it is easy. But for first-timers, it is a nightmare. First we must get into the correct lane and approach the correct booth—and there are many—otherwise we will be locked into a situation our nerves cannot cope with.

Some of the lanes are for regular autostrada users with Telepass cards. These drivers simply flash their cards at a machine and the tollgate goes up. Other lanes have slots for money, slits for credit cards and complicated (to us) buttons to push to receive a ticket and make the gate go up. Get in the wrong lane with the wrong card or incorrect money or no credit card, and the gate will not go up.

Think about this for a moment, please. We are locked in. We have, by now, at least half a dozen impatient Italian racing-car drivers behind us revving their engines, blowing their horns and waving their fists. The gate will not open. We cannot go forward. We cannot go back. This little situation needs no further explanation, does it?

Several wrong lanes, firmly locked gates and many angry drivers later, we learn to approach tollbooths with great scrutiny before we dare choose a lane. The credit card slots are the worst. Each time we insert the card we pray to the Madonna we have just cursed that our card will come out again, but of course it never does. This may have something to do with the fact that we have not inserted a ticket with it, but we are not to know this at the time. It isn't until our fifth attempt, and following many raised fingers from our fellow drivers, that we realise there is a little speaker on the side of the booth for us to talk to someone, get advice, get help.

But pressing the button and receiving a snappy '*Pronto?*,' doesn't inspire confidence. We doubt the faceless person is going to understand my shrill 'Help me get the hell out of this mess!', but somehow she does and, shortly thereafter, a uniformed woman appears magically from a field of sunflowers by the road, comes over to us and fiddles with things until the gate goes up and we go through, once again vowing never to drive in Italy.

Twelve

Capri. We have been counting first the years until we could get to this beautiful island, then the months, then the weeks and now the days, because finally we have made it to Sorrento and will spend one night here before taking the ferry to Capri.

But first we must find a place to stay in Sorrento, and I must tell you a little about the place. Sorrento looks exactly how Bill Bryson described in it his marvellous book *Neither Here Nor There*. (Funny that, one of the world's most popular travel writers describing places accurately.) It is full of middle-aged touristy couples on cheap holidays from the UK, filling the streets, cafés and bars, always prattling on and on about nothing. We pass one in a little street off the small and lovely Piazza Tasso, her stridently telling an elegant Italian shopkeeper with an elegant shop full of elegant shoes behind him, 'I'll give you fifteen quid for these sandals, not a penny more. Take it or leave it'. Bargaining as though she were on the streets of Bangkok, she is so typical of everything we scorn, yet we often see in ourselves, that it makes us shudder. We scurry away from her as quickly as possible, only to pass another couple bargaining in a souvenir shop, and another, and another. Nothing makes us cringe quite like seeing a fellow traveller/countryman do something that looks and sounds horribly awkward in a foreign country. We, of course, behave beautifully at all times and adjust to local cultures with alacrity. And we never lie, either.

There are some gorgeous hotels in Sorrento, which sits on the edge of the cliff that tumbles down into the beautiful Bay of Naples. We wander into elegant reception lobbies to inquire about prices and peer through to fabulous gardened pool areas where well-fed guests bask in expensive bathing suits on comfortable deck chairs, drinks and books close to hand. After finding all of these hotels way out of our stingy price range, we stumble into the Lorerley Hotel, a 'cute, family-run hotel' (as my notes now tell me) tucked in beside the swanky places on the front. It is well priced and, although nothing flash (the toilet takes up every bit of bathroom space and the shower is almost directly above it), has very pretty gardens and an alfresco restaurant overlooking the most— and I really do mean *the most*—spectacular views out over the Bay of Naples. We notice later that these views are the ones used on most of Sorrento's postcards and brochures. We quickly dub the Lorerley Hotel the Loverly Hotel because, apart from the small bathroom, it really is.

We are too enamoured of the hotel's gardens and the view to bother with a reconnoitre of the town, so we decide to stay put. Even though it is just two in the afternoon, we order a small bottle of wine and sit at a table in the sunshine feeling smug and content. Hundreds of metres below is a small beach where suntanned people sit on a long jetty over the clear blue sea and occasionally jump in and splash about. The small bottle of wine disappears in two or three minutes and puts us in a self-satisfied mood. So much beauty calls for another bottle of wine—a big one this time—and we sip and tell each other we will go down to that water below and join those brown people and jump off that jetty and swim ... after this next glass. The hotel has its own small lift that will take us down there.

An hour later, we are almost drunk; just as well, too, because under sober conditions nothing on earth would have induced me to get into that lift. I have an aversion to lifts at the best of times, when they are located in the most efficient of places and contain an emergency phone with an English-speaking person on the other end. So, when a small clunking private lift in an Italian family-run hotel actually travels a few hundred metres slowly down through solid rock, I would ordinarily tend to get a bit nervous. Visions of being entombed inside a cliff for days without an emergency phone, praying someone above was doing something about it, would have brought me undone, but the wine bravery sees me hurtling enthusiastically into the small tomb with four fat men, one of them being my Geoffrey.

Slowly, slowly, slowly, down, down, down we go. The five of us hold in our breath and stomachs and I pray fervently that nothing will make this lift stop inside the cliff. The god of lifts is listening to me and we all fall out many minutes later at the bottom—red, hot and so very relieved. We immediately plunge into the cool water and after an hour of swimming have sobered up completely and must face the tomb again, for there is no other way to get back up the cliff. Eyes shut, praying again, we inch our way up and (thank you, God, for listening to me once again) make it up to the hotel without incident, but nothing will ever get me inside that lift again. And if you happen to find yourself in Sorrento one day, seek out the Lorerley Hotel, check out that lift and see if the hairs on the back of your neck don't stand on end.

We so want to have dinner in the hotel's garden terrace surrounded by the tubs of geraniums and watch the sun set over the Bay of Naples, but the restaurant is fully booked, so we walk into the small *piazza* and wander around the shops before making our way through the exciting network of atmospheric narrow streets leading off the *piazza*. We find a large, busy outdoor café and take a seat, along with a crowd watching a football match between England and Romania on a television in the corner. We eat spaghetti, veal and steak and drink two bottles of red wine (God, we can put it away) and watch the crowd watching the football. They are engrossed, cheering and clapping loudly, and it is impossible not to enjoy their enjoyment. I try to imagine a similar scene in Australia—me sitting in a pub watching a crowd of blokes watching the footy, and me actually enjoying it—but I can't quite capture the vision.

We stroll back through the alleyways, looking at brightly lit interesting shops, all open late into the night, all without a single customer, all with bored shopkeepers standing in the doorways. We wander into surely the best *gelato* shop in the world. Its long refrigerated cabinets have every flavour of *gelato* imaginable, from bright green kiwifruit to a dozen varieties of chocolate, including Mars Bar and Snickers. I could stay in here for hours just looking, but Geoffrey is bored and reminds me of my ever-expanding waistline, which makes me scuttle quickly out of temptation's way.

Back at the Loverly Hotel, sitting on the toilet having a shower before bed, I decide that this has been one of the nicest and easiest days I can remember and if I wasn't so in love with Santa Margherita, I'd fall head over heels for Sorrento.

A breakfast of outstanding awfulness—tasteless bread rolls and lukewarm mud masquerading as coffee—in the gorgeous terrace restaurant does not make for a good start to the following day, but food really isn't important when we are finally about to get to Capri. Our ferry is not due to leave until midday, so we decide a morning ride on the bus along the Amalfi Coast is a rather splendid idea. Just about everyone has seen pictures of the Amalfi Coast, the fabulous hotels, houses and apartment buildings all carved into the rock face overlooking the Bay of Naples with impossibly beautiful views. We are about to see it first-hand.

We race to the crowded bus just as it is about to depart and leap on, only to find we need pre-paid tickets. The driver stares at us blankly and then indicates a ticket box many metres away across the road. Geoffrey runs back to buy tickets while everyone on the bus waits. For a few nervous minutes everyone is patient, even the driver, but as more minutes pass with no sign of Geoffrey, discontented mumblings start and quickly turn into aggravated shouts. It is one of the only times I am glad I don't understand much of the Italian language. Just as fists and fingers are about to be raised in my direction, Geoffrey comes panting back, everyone goes quiet and we take off. The bus is ridiculously over-crowded; we are standing up at the front with dozens of bodies pressing into us, but discomfort is a minor thing when we consider that this ride on this route on this bus has to be one of the cheapest and most outstandingly fabulous tours in Italy, if not the world. For a minimal bus fare, we are taken around tight, narrow, winding roads and treated to a scenic drive as thrilling as anything you could find anywhere on earth.

People are squashed and clinging to the straps, but that doesn't stop the passengers reaching out and hanging their video cameras out of the window to capture some of this fabulousness. Each time a bus approaches from the opposite direction there is much horn blowing, fist waving and stubborn refusals from both drivers to back up, but after a tense stand-off they slowly start to inch past each other, only millimetres of space between them.

Just before we reach Positano, an overweight man pushes and shoves his way to the front of the bus; not a single *scusa* does he utter as he shoulders and elbows people to get past. In German-accented English, he demands the bus driver make an unscheduled stop in the middle of the road, but the driver will have none of it. The German remains standing by the driver, glaring and muttering. Minutes later, when we make our official stop at Positano and all trundle off at this unbelievably pretty place, the German unzips his fly and pees against a bougainvillaea-lined wall. No wonder he wanted the bus to stop urgently. I could have kicked him in his testicles, which wouldn't have been difficult seeing as he'd left his fly open and they were peeking out at me. I know this alfresco peeing is a European thing; I know some French men think nothing of unzipping anywhere at any time; but really, in front of a busload of people in one of the most beautiful places in the world? What has happened to us?

We walk down many flights of steps through Positano's lovely narrow streets, passing shops of great gorgeousness right down to the beach. We watch the rich people sitting on expensive sun lounges and decide this place is as close to heaven as we could ask for. (Mind you, we say that about every place we visit in Italy, from Siena to Lucca to Pisa to Sorrento to Capri to Positano … we go crazy with love, dumb with awe.) After an age of staring at the fascinating scene, we wander back up and get a seat on an almost-empty bus and enjoy the spectacular ride back, this time in comfort.

Australian friends holidaying in Italy at the same time as us have done almost the same itinerary, but are a few weeks ahead of us at each stop. When we were in Santa Margherita, they were on Capri and had telephoned us, gushing and raving about the island.

'It's fabulous; full of beautiful people and gorgeous things and wonderful views', they said. 'And the shops! Wait until you see the shops.' But then: 'It's beautiful, but expensive, really expensive. Everything is expensive. Whatever you do, don't let the porters take your bags up to your hotel from the ferry. It cost us a hundred dollars just to have our bags delivered to our hotel'. A hundred dollars just to have a couple of bags delivered to a hotel? Unthinkable.

So, after the ferry docks at Marina Grande on Capri and we reject the services of seventy-five taxi drivers and several hundred porters, we take off on foot to the funicular, trundling our two big suitcases and one large hand case. The queue for tickets is typical of all Italian queues—messy, squashed and full of pushy tourists— but this time we are just as pushy and get our tickets after only a fifteen-minute wait and squeeze our way onto the funicular. As we ride up the hill, we laugh and congratulate ourselves on saving the porter's outlandish fee. It was uncomfortable lugging the big bags onto the funicular while everyone gave us dark looks, but it wasn't really very difficult.

Tumbling into Piazza Umberto I with heavy cases and hundreds of other people isn't exactly the way we want to arrive in the famous *piazza* and there is no chance to absorb the first impact of its charm, but we don't mind. We have weeks here to let it steal our hearts, and our most urgent task is to find our hotel and get rid of our bags. Down the narrow cobblestoned streets off the main square we trudge, pulling our heavy cases behind us. Past lovely small shops full of designer names we walk and walk, looking for our hotel, which I shall call the Villa Fabulous in case the owner ever reads this, recognises herself in the not-so-flattering light in which I am about to portray her and bans me forever from coming back to her lovely place.

There has been much lead-up to this booking at the Villa Fabulous. A friend who visits Capri regularly has sought it out for us and told us it is in a good position, with great views down to the Bay of Naples. Many telephone calls from Australia to the fearsome-sounding Signora have secured us a room at a big price, but no matter how many times I have asked on the telephone for assurance that our room has a view, she will not commit. I have imagined us in this lovely place, perched high on the cliffs with the best position in Capri and, while all the other guests sit and gloat at the front on balconies overlooking the sea, we are stuck in a dingy back room, facing the rubbish bin area.

On and on we walk, sweating and puffing heavily as we search for Villa Fabulous. We finally ask someone for directions, only to find we have been walking the wrong way. Back we turn, retracing our steps and then coming to a narrow winding footpath that leads past more beautiful shops and stunning views.

Up narrow steps … around tight corners … up more steps … up yet more and more … and still more … and … finally, we can see the Villa Fabulous, white, sparkling and surrounded by pink geraniums high up on the hill. At least a hundred more steps to climb. Panting as though our hearts will burst, we climb up and up, sweating and cursing the greedy people who could charge a hundred dollar porter's fee. After many stops to double over in agony and wait for our laboured breathing to slow, we arrive at Villa Fabulous and stagger into a small reception area to find the formidable Signora sitting straightbacked at a desk. There is no mistaking her: small, elegant, stern, scary and, right now, perplexed at seeing two big, sweating, panting Australians on her doorstep.

'Why did you not call for a porter?' she asks coolly, looking at us as though we are completely unhinged. 'We have a free service.'

After we cool down and off, after the Signora has completed her bits of paperwork, after I have asked her at least five times if our room has a view and after she has not condescended to answer, she hands us a key with a wooden tag the size of a wardrobe and takes us up another flight of stairs. By now I am too intimidated to speak and will accept any cockroach-infested hole in the wall she might care to give us. But she shows us into a room of dazzling loveliness with a view of unbelievable beauty, then gives us a smug 'all-of-my-rooms-are-bloody-fantastic-you-ignorant-Australians' look and departs quietly. Overcome with gratitude at our good fortune and weak from all the step-climbing, we throw ourselves onto the bed, unable to speak.

Later, we explore our room. Spacious and spotless, it has a patterned tiled floor, a wrought-iron bed, a small antique table and desk and comfortable chairs; more than enough for our needs. The distinctive floor tiles continue into the spacious bathroom, where we are relieved to find the toilet a good distance away from the shower. Outside is a big blue-tiled terrace with lounge chairs and a table with a pink tablecloth. And the views—oh God, our views—are surely the best on Capri. Out over the sparkling water (I hate describing water as sparkling all the time, but it really does sparkle in the sunlight and there isn't any other way to describe it, apart from shimmering, it shimmers too) to the famous Faraglioni, the two giant rocks synonymous with Capri that rise out of the sea, we have endless beauty before us. One of the Faraglioni has a big hole in the middle, which small boats constantly pass through. Much has been written about the Faraglioni; thousands of people have gaped in wonder at them, but nothing can really prepare us for seeing their soaring splendour from our own balcony and knowing they are ours to wonder at, if only temporarily. Way below us is a flat, tiled lookout space at the end of a small road. This place receives hundreds of daytrippers every day to take in this marvellous view. There is a constant trek of them from dawn until dusk, but fortunately for us they do not all come at once and are far enough below us to be out of earshot. We can, however, see them taking thousands of photos and gazing dreamily at the view that is theirs for just a few minutes, but ours twenty-four hours a day.

It is early afternoon when we check in, but because this is such an out-of-our-normal-holiday-experience occasion, we call for wine to celebrate. The only flaw of this lovely Villa Fabulous is that all the rooms facing this remarkable view share one long balcony, the only privacy coming from a thin bit of see-through netting separating each space. This simply will not do. I cannot sit on my balcony guzzling wine while someone just a metre or two away can watch. We drape our towels over the see-through screen, which gives a little more privacy but not enough, so Geoffrey calls for some of my size sixteen sundresses to act as temporary tarpaulins. Under normal circumstances this would lead to something ugly but I am drunk with wine and glee so simply drape my big fat dresses over the flimsy barrier and flop down smugly to enjoy it all.

In the early evening, we explore. Our first stop is Piazza Umberto I, the famous *piazza* that features in books, postcards, brochures and anything else that depicts Capri. It is irresistible. We promise to look through the church at one end later, which of course we don't because, as you will read later, we are too busy in the pursuit of food, wine and other indulgences to get back to it. But, if you're interested, it was the Santo Stefano seventeenth-century church, and I highly recommend that, should you find yourselves on the bewitching island of Capri one day, explore it. For now, the busy cafés lining the square—all with outdoor tables and chairs and attractive waiters in lemon jackets and navy blue ties serving gorgeous people—are calling us.

A waiter who looks as though he has stepped off the set of 'The Bold and Beautiful' serves us a gin-and-tonic and a beer. Dark and handsome, suave and debonair, he serves our drinks and then bestows, from a small silver tray, complimentary little dishes of nibblies. As always, these are presented with elaborate gestures and great pride, but when we dip into them we discover they are nothing more than little cubes of hard bread and a few stale potato chips. It has been the same in bars all over Italy. The manner in which waiters present these fusty bits and pieces with such self-assurance impresses me immensely. I vow to do the same the next time I entertain back at home. I'll put a handful of Cheezles and Twisties into my little Carrara marble bowls, place them on a silver tray and then do a small sweep-through-the-air gesture before placing them reverently before my guests as though they are bowls of Beluga caviar and rare black truffles. Perhaps I'll add a little curtsey as I offer them, just to reinforce their importance.

After our drinks, we join the masses of other holiday-makers and stroll through Capri's lovely pedestrian cobblestoned streets, stopping to look in the divine shops, which are Aladdin's caves full of gifts, jewels, clothes and shoes—shoes so indescribably beautiful I can't describe them.

There is just one road on Capri, winding from Marina Grande to the top of the rocky cliffs and then on to Anacapri on the other side of the island. The island must be explored on foot along a network of bewitching flower-lined streets and pedestrianised paths. We are awed by this place and can't really take it all in.

Later we wander into an elaborate restaurant, near our Villa Fabulous and with the same spectacular views and an abundance of terracotta-potted pink geraniums. The waiters tell us off mildly for not making a booking and brag about how busy they are, even though the place is half-empty at this stage. They give us the worst table, near the kitchen door, and serve us over-salted and over-priced spaghetti and a bottle of wine. Their brochure boasts of regular visits from Pavarotti and other famous people, who obviously like views when they eat out, not good food (although this is perhaps not entirely true of Pavarotti).

The following morning we sit in the sun on Villa Fabulous's blue-tiled breakfast terrace, which is directly below our room's own terrace and is surrounded by terracotta pots of pale lavender hydrangeas and pink geraniums. As we eat sugary croissants with cream cheese and jam, we overlook the sea and the Faraglioni and cannot believe our good fortune. Apart from the Signora glaring at us from just inside the door, it is all so very perfect.

Afterwards we want to walk. We must see and get to know every centimetre of this lovely island. We begin at the narrow road behind the Villa Fabulous and climb up past old stone walls covered in vines, hiding large luxurious villas. We try to peek through heavy gates and ornate carved doors but everything is camouflaged beneath masses of bougainvillea and geraniums. We walk so high that the views to Marina Piccola and the blue sea in the distance way below appear small.

We can see Anacapri far away on the other side of the island and decide to walk there in the afternoon. We go back to the information centre in Piazza Umberto I to inquire if it is a dangerous walk; it certainly looks perilous from way up on top of the island. The road twists and winds its way dangerously high with frighteningly long drops on one side way down to the rocks and ocean.

'No, not dangerous at all', the woman in the information centre says, so off we trot trustingly. Whether she is new or deliberately wants us dead we will never know, but she certainly almost gets us killed. We climb and climb along the road, sticking to the side where the high wall of the mountain offers a little protection, looking out to the other side of the road where the drop is sheer and terrifying. As we near the top, the road becomes very narrow and big buses full of people spilling out of doors and hanging out of windows charge down the hill, missing us by centimetres. At one stage we have to press ourselves flat against the cliff face to avoid being hit. If we had been on the other side of the road, the 300-metre drop down to the ocean that I keep telling you is sparkling would have been the only place to leap to get out of the way of the buses. Only Italian bus drivers could make their big vehicles squeeze past each other on such tight bends and narrow roads.

Just as we become really frightened, we come across a set of incredibly steep stairs carved into the mountain, which obviously lead right up to outer space. They are the most daunting steps we have ever seen but at this stage we will do anything to get off this dangerous road, so we take to them. They are so steep we have to press our hands to our thighs to hoist ourselves up. We can see people at what appears to be a church floating in the sky high above us, so we press on, huffing and puffing, until we come across several hundred tourists crammed into a flat terrace in front of a small church. We have arrived at Anacapri. The tourists stare shamelessly at us; some congratulate us upon hearing we have walked all the way up on that hideously dangerous road from Capri. None can believe we have done such a stupid, life-threatening thing.

Being a couple that rarely does much research before embarking on anything as big as a holiday or as small as a walk, we do not realise we have just walked up the famous Phoenician steps, built into the rock face in ancient times. As we wander into the pretty town of Anacapri, we see art galleries full of paintings and prints of these famous steps; every small shop has postcards depicting them. We are shamed by our ignorance. Later, when we read about the Phoenician steps, we learn that in ancient times it was nothing for the locals to run up and down these steps many dozens of times a day with huge bundles on their heads. Once, bundle-free, had almost finished us.

Anacapri stretches out at the foot of Mount Solaro and covers a plateau jewelled with vineyards and olive trees. It is the second, smaller community on the island and just as lovely as Capri, but in a less flamboyant way. And everything here seems half the price. The action centres on Piazza della Vittoria, a terminal for those big buses as well as the cable car to Mount Solaro. We have had more than enough heights for one day, so we give the cable car a miss and have a modest lunch—without wine for a change—in a gardened courtyard we have been enticed into by a spruiker in the doorway.

'Our food is the best in Anacapri', the woman tells us, first in German (this happens to us a lot; we obviously look like a couple of big, well-fed Germans), then in English. She lied, of course. A tiny dish of tasteless gnocchi, an even smaller one of flavourless cannelloni, fifty dollars and five minutes later, we are ready to go back to Capri.

'A taxi back', I plead. 'I couldn't face that road again.'

We are ripped off by the taxi driver who, after lying like the spruiker and saying his was the best taxi on the island, charges us twenty-five dollars for a five dollar ride. But it is only our second day on Capri and we don't mind. Let these people dare to try to part us from our money tomorrow.

With this in mind, we search for that rarity in Italy, a free beach. I think every town is obliged to provide a handkerchief-sized square of pebbles for the hoi polloi, so we know there has to be at least one beach without a man with a money bag waiting to take twenty dollars from us. And we do find one. It is minuscule and packed past capacity, but free. We compress our bums into a few centimetres of unoccupied space and sit bolt upright to watch the action around us.

A couple of beautiful models are in the middle of a photo shoot. She is gorgeous in a silvery green see-through shift with a tiny green bikini underneath; he is splendid with slicked back hair, smooth olive skin, a deadly white smile and a tight pair of Speedos. The photographer has them posing in each other's arms in the water, then lying on a wide flat rock in the water, then her sprawling at the water's edge and then crawling out of the sea. It is very sexy, especially when her wet see-through shift plasters against her body, and even more so with the stunning background of the Faraglioni. The shoot goes on for hours and entertains us throughout the afternoon.

At one stage, a wonderfully enormous woman in a huge blue bathing suit accidentally wanders into the background of the photo shoot. She stands hippo-like behind the models, arms splashing into the water, blissfully unaware that she is ruining an ultra-glamorous scene. The camera crew are the epitome of politeness, waiting until she has had her fun and is ready to move out of camera range. It makes me laugh out loud with pleasure, and it is only Geoffrey's strong grip that prevents me from getting up and wandering into the background myself to further spoil the sexy scene.

It is obvious after two days that we are not going to stick to our budget on Capri. Every time we stop for a coffee, a drink, bottles of water, we seem to be about a hundred dollars lighter. Our room has no kitchen facilities, so all meals have to be taken in expensive restaurants, but putting together a snack on our balcony could be possible.

With this in mind, we buy dense bread, tomatoes on the vine and gorgonzola from a jolly, chubby man in a tiny deli in a backstreet. He offers us a bottle of his own wine for five dollars and we can't believe our luck. Five dollars for wine? On Capri? Incredible. But when we take our first sip back on our balcony, congratulating ourselves on our budget-minded approach, we see instantly why it is cheap—it is a foul and poisonous concoction, more suitable for cleaning drains than drinking.

This is the first time we have stopped since arriving on Capri, and it is time to read up about this dazzling place. It's okay for me to go on and on about shimmering seas and sparkling oceans and to-die-for shoes and expensive spaghetti and luxurious villas and terracotta pots of pink geraniums, but I am sure you would like to know a bit about Capri's history and geography.

Capri is on the outermost southern point of the Gulf of Naples. Despite two thousand years of people flocking to this bewitching island—think about that, two thousand years of tourism—it has managed to maintain its awesome beauty and a feeling of untainted nature. I have no idea how.

Every day during the height of the summer season a succession of ferries from Naples and Sorrento spews out thousands of tourists at Marina Grande. We make the mistake of getting caught up in a particularly large vomit one day down at the port and are locked in, backed up tightly against a brick wall for half an hour as a choking stream of people pours out onto the wharf. It is genuinely frightening to be so clogged in by such a vast mass of people. It is so congested, nobody can walk; they have to shuffle as if in leg chains, a few centimetres at a time, shoulder to shoulder, fronts pressed against backs, boobs pressed against shoulders, pelvises pushed against buttocks. And this is just one ferry-load of people that gets off and up onto the funicular and into Capri's narrow streets. Multiply this by forty or more, and you have thousands and thousands of people coming onto the island each day. Thank goodness the day visitors leave after dark and the island quietens down—a little.

Capri is formed mostly of limestone, and its brown cliff faces certainly don't look exciting from the distance. But on the island, the cliffs overhang and give the feeling of being suspended above the water (sparkling, of course). The cliffs are honeycombed with grottoes and gorges, which are easily explorable by a (frighteningly expensive) hire boat. Capri's main industry is, as you discerning readers will have guessed, tourism, but there is a bit of agriculture going on—the island abounds in olive groves—and some fishing as well. Lemon trees are everywhere, lovely green things full of plump fruit and bright yellow cheer. This area of southern Italy is the home of Limoncello, of which we will be drinking copious amounts over the coming weeks.

Capri has countless little paths to explore, never-ending historic villas to look at, everlasting ruins to ramble over, innumerable cafés to sit in, limitless views to sigh over, masses of flowers to smell and endless sea to cool off in. Tourism is nothing new to Capri; the island's captivating charms lured both Julius and Tiberius Caesar to build summer villas here, and millions of excited tourists like us have followed ever since.

When the famous and fabulous Grand Hotel Quisisana was built on Capri in 1845, the builders discovered implements belonging to the late Paleolithic Stone Age. The island's volcanoes were still active then and the island was joined to the continent. There is evidence of human settlement dating back long before records were even thought of, let alone kept, on the island. Its most interesting and more recent history—well, when I say recent, I mean AD 26–37—was when the wicked bad boy Tiberius made the island his residence, from where he governed the whole Roman Empire. The dissolute Emperor alternated his governing duties with erotic diversions involving adolescents of both sexes. When he was bored with his lovers or houseguests, he tortured them until he got bored with that too, then had them thrown from the cliffs to die horribly on the rocks below. And who could blame him, because if you were to be really frank with me, isn't that pretty much what you'd like to do to ex-lovers and annoying houseguests when you tire of them?

The Grand Hotel Quisisana is far too fabulous for us to contemplate even having a drink in. But we do take a stroll through its sumptuous foyer one evening after many glasses of wine have given us the courage to step inside. The hotel is almost as synonymous with Capri as the Blue Grotto is, and has seen royalty, actors, writers, industrialists and jet-setters inside its lovely rooms. The names of famous people who have stayed here are too many to list, but if I were to mention Tom Cruise ... James Belushi ... Duran Duran ... Ernest Hemingway ... would you be impressed? I was.

Each week on Capri we count down, trying to milk the days for the best of every hour that slips by too quickly. We know we are living a dream and will have to pay for this in ways other than monetary when we get home. We are convinced we will be punished in some way for experiencing so much pleasure. The guilt grows each day as we idle our time away with trashy books on our sunny balcony, as we sit in cafés high on the cliffs and watch the sky change slowly from vivid blue to sun-streaked mauve to burnished orange, and the sea turn into liquid gold (sparkling gold). As we cradle late-night Limoncellos in our hands and look back out on hills to thousands of twinkling lights, we are certain there will have to be a later forfeit, a sacrifice for this much pleasure.

I ask Geoffrey to walk me long distances every day. 'Set off and I'll follow', I tell him, because not only are our waistlines expanding alarmingly, the walks are so inspiring they reveal yet more and more beauty at each turn. This day we set off, complete with hats, water bottles, backpacks, good shoes and a map, and tramp past high stone walls with thick ivy hiding elaborate villas, and smaller walls we can see over to grounds full of grapevines and lemon trees. We reach L'Arco Naturale, an incredible rock formation jutting high up out of the sea and shaped in a natural arch. L'Arco Naturale is what is left of a huge limestone cave eroded by wind and rain over a million years. It is one of the best backdrops for a photo you are likely to come across. We are so high at this point that we are actually higher than nesting birds, and the feeling is both exhilarating and frightening. The urge to leap off, to fly out over the sea like the wild birds is compelling. Fortunately, we restrain ourselves.

We walk up the Via Tiberio to the Villa Jovis—where the bad boy emperor Tiberius did all his partying and torturing and killing— and refuse to pay an old man four thousand lire (four dollars) each just to go and look at the ruins. Later, we walk down the hill and come across a little restaurant named La Savardina among the lemon groves, where we enjoy a cup of coffee and a slice of chocolate torte beneath lemon trees heavy with the fattest lemons we've ever seen. With the effects of the latte, we regret not paying to look at the ruins. We should have tramped over the ruins, got more of a feel for the debauchery that went on there. This is the largest and best preserved of the Roman villas on the island. Maybe we would have gained a real feel for the beautiful villa, the grand halls and the vast rooms, the baths and gardens, if only we hadn't been so tight-fisted. We make a promise to come back.

We continue our walk, map in hand, going down now, down steep steps, along narrow tracks, always with views to the water hundreds of metres below us. By now we are hot and desperate to cool off, but each turn takes us off in a direction away from the water. We ask young girls coming the other way if they have come up from the sea, but they do not speak English. We pass a group of German teenage boys eating a picnic of massive salami, slabs of bread and tiny cherry tomatoes on the side of the track. 'Have you come up from the water?' we ask anxiously, but they are too interested in their salami and teasing each other to give us a coherent answer. We then come across a group of young Italian men cavorting on the path and we ask them the way. Although they don't speak a word of English, they are happy to babble and give us incomprensible directions. Eventually the path begins to drop very steeply and the water becomes enticingly close.

We come to a restaurant on the water's edge with its own private roped-off beach. There is no way to get to the beach other than through the restaurant and it is obvious that we will have to eat in the restaurant if we want to use the water. We don't want to pay for an expensive lunch just to be able to take a dip in the sea, so we ask someone coming out if there is a public place for swimming.

Absolutely not, is the reply. So, if we want to get wet, we will have to pay. We walk up again, then down, and come to another restaurant on the rocks, also with its own roped-off glorious beach at its feet. We have two options: have lunch and swim as part of the deal, or pay the twenty dollars each to sit on the rocks by the water. We grumble angrily to each other as we reluctantly pay a small, over-tanned old man wearing a bit of anal floss as swimwear. Forty dollars just to enjoy a swim in free water. It's outrageous. But we get a deckchair and a locker and when we slip down into the cool green water (not so sparkling close-up) it is worth it. The water restores our spirits, cools our tempers and brings us back to life after our three-hour walk.

All around us, mature women sprawl on the rocks or in deckchairs, their faces to the sun, bikini tops abandoned, necks wrinkled and crêped, saggy boobs burnt black. They fascinate me. Their weathered bodies give lie to the sun/cancer connection, but how they can think such sun-punished skin is attractive is beyond imagination. Many wear g-string bikini bottoms, and the sight of a slip of material disappearing between scrawny buttocks holds my attention for so long, I half-expect the ticket man to come and charge me another twenty dollars for the freaky peep show.

After a few hours on the rocks—and not until we feel we have had full value for our money—we wander back up to the restaurant, now almost empty after a busy lunchtime. We discover we have already booked at this place for the following Sunday, but after a gin-and-tonic served by a surly waiter and a look at the ordinary menu, we cancel. We linger and listen to a group of Italian men sitting in tiny swimming trunks and playing cards at a table behind. They appear to be arguing fiercely while laughing at the same time; it's fascinating and quite marvellous.

We are dreading the long walk back, so are thrilled when our grumpy waiter tells us we can get a boat back for three thousand lire (about three dollars). We return to the Villa Fabulous and sit until late in the evening on our balcony and assess our financial situation. This day has been relatively cheap, but has still cost us about a hundred and fifty dollars in little incidentals—this is without lunch or dinner, just our tomatoes and bread on our balcony. We are stricken with guilt at this excess, and I tell Geoffrey this is actually a good thing. This relentless guilt is to be our punishment for enjoying ourselves so much and will surely look after us and save us from a far worse fate.

We discover the Via Krupp, a spectacular, sinuous pedestrian road that a German magnate named Friedrich Krupp built early last century so he could more easily reach his boat anchored at Marina Piccola from the Quisisana, where he lived, the lucky bastard. Wouldn't it be something to be so rich that you could build your own road just for the convenience of getting from one luxurious thing to another? And not just a plain old road, but something so outstanding that it would become an icon bearing your name. You have to see Via Krupp to absorb its full and spectacular impact. It has been called the world's most beautiful road (probably by the engineer who built it) and it really is something special. It hugs the cliffs and coils around on itself so that you are constantly looking up or down at it. We pose on its low walls—well, I do at least—and now have several dozen decidedly unglamorous shots of me thinking I look ultra glamorous. This panoramic road unites Capri with the waterfront of Marina Piccola below, winding thrillingly past the cobalt sea dotted with yachts. For some reason the top of the road is now gated and locked, but as it is an excellent short cut for us to get to Marina Piccola, we climb awkwardly over the gate and head down this intriguing road. On many of the anchored yachts we pass, people sit and eat and drink and jump into the beautiful sea. It makes us sick with envy.

There is a broad clump of large flat rocks jutting into the sea down off the Via Krupp; people are lying on these rocks and swimming in the sea, *with no-one there collecting money*. This is obviously a free spot, and with good reason; it is almost impossible to get to unless you are young and fit. We, as you will have gathered, are neither, but a free beach is a big incentive for a crash course in weight loss and increased fitness levels. Geoffrey scrambles down, clearing a little path for me lumbering inelegantly behind him. It is very difficult, but we make it, scratched and sweating, cursing this bloody beach-payment thing that forces middle-aged, overweight morons to find free space in difficult-to-get-to spots.

Some thoughtful person has erected a small ladder on one of the rocks, which is good, because once I jump into the water, I have no chance of hoisting my big bulk back up. We swim happily for hours, the water like soft, cool silk on our skin.

But someone—perhaps one of those lucky rich bastards jumping off the yachts—has thrown plastic bags, empty juice and soft drink bottles, apple cores, orange peel, plastic cups and cigarette butts into the water. They are caught together on a gentle current and float past me on a long, slim rubbish stream. I am shocked. How anyone can have such blatant disregard for this perfection astounds me and makes me want to get out of the water, find out who is responsible and rip their hearts out.

As I swim along pondering this violent thought and avoiding the crap, there floats before me something far worse than all the above. Right before my nose, gliding along as cheerfully as though it were on a Sunday outing, is a *panty shield*. Good God, if I was shocked by the cigarette packets and orange peel, I can't tell you what this little number does to me. I am later to find these panty shields floating about all over the place. Whole flotillas of them gather in the currents and swim by me almost every day. Obviously women (and quite possibly a few of the blokes) visiting Capri this season wear these little things in their swimsuits and they come adrift in the water and sail their merry way all over the sea.

I think I'll end this chapter on that savoury note.

Thirteen

Shoes. Italy. Shoes. Need I say more? Yes, I think I must.

But before I start ranting on, it must be said that Geoffrey is a kind and patient man. However, in the manner of almost every other heterosexual man in the world, he is not fond of shopping. He tries. Sometimes he even pretends. He will stand outside a shop and not say anything while I pop in for a browse, but his body language is that of a long-suffering martyr and makes it impossible for me to linger enjoyably over a purchase.

Geoffrey holds on tightly to his wallet when it comes to shopping and has the uncanny knack of bringing up the subject of our diminishing funds at the most inappropriate moments. We might be sitting in a pretty little café surrounded by pots of geraniums and other loveliness and, just as I begin to raise my coffee cup to my lips, he will start to slowly shake his head morosely and say something like, 'Do you realise it's going to take us two years to pay our credit cards off after this?'. It somehow ruins the moment.

At the end of each perfect afternoon in Italy, as we pull up a chair to celebrate the *aperitivi* hour, he opens his wallet, peers into it with a look of pitiful anxiety and says, 'Cor, you really go through the money here, don't you?'. Actually, he doesn't say 'cor'; I just made that up. He really says something far earthier, which I won't repeat because I don't want you to think too badly of Geoffrey.

And this brings me back to the subject of shoes. In Italy exist the most beautiful shoes on the planet. Strappy pink sandals ... pale blue snakeskin boots ... flirty black stilettos ... little green mules ... shoes with tiny fragile flowers on them ... shoes with diamantés on the toes ... shoes with cut-out mesh bits ... shoes with every conceivable kind of bauble, trinket and pompom on them to make a girl's heart sing and an old sheila's heart yearn. Italy's shoes have soles that any woman would gladly trade her soul for.

But here's the thing: I have big fat size ten bunioned feet, and every one of these sensational shoes would look like a navy battleship on me. (Presuming, of course, that I could squeeze into any of them, which I can't.) But this doesn't stop me standing at windows drooling with desire to own a pair of these wanton things. In a stupid moment of wistful yearning, I admit to Geoffrey that, although I would gladly swap my old mother for any pair of these sexy shoes, I have no hope of ever squeezing my fat hoofers into them. This brightens Geoffrey up no end. Suddenly I find myself being cheerfully steered towards every shoe shop in Capri by a man who has never in three-plus decades of marriage shown any interest in what goes on my feet. I can feel his confidence as he points out a pair of small pale lemon leather thongs with a three-digit price tag. I can almost see his chest swell as he looks at a tiny pair of indecently wicked pink sandals and asks if I want to try them on—'go ahead, go on, try them on, go on, I'll wait'.

It is the same at the understated but hallowed Prada and Gucci stores. Ever since I stupidly announced that the past few spaghetti-filled weeks had shot me up at least another five kilos and made even the dreadful size sixteens feel tight, I have been dragged towards every strapless, frothy, sequined, slinky frock in Italy.

'That would be good on you', Geoffrey says, pointing to a size eight lacy shift dress in Gucci. 'See if it fits. I'll wait.' I will get him back for this day.

Actually, my opportunity for revenge comes sooner rather than later. On one of the enchanting narrow streets filled with souvenir shops and galleries, we come across a man sitting on a small stool outside a shoe shop, hand-making shoes. His worktable is covered with instruments and soles of every size, onto which he is stitching, gluing and hammering straps and bits of black and tan leather and glittering froufrous. Lovely shoes are being created before our eyes for a long line of eager customers. His tiny shop is packed tightly from floor to ceiling with shelves of soles and glitzy accessories. One thing is obvious: anything could be possible here, even something girly and hot-diggity for my big feet. I have to wait in line for quite a while to chat with Franco, which is what I'll call him because I've forgotten his real name. By the time it is my turn to sit opposite Franco at his small crowded table, Geoffrey is well into martyr mode, as he well deserves to be for taunting me in all those lovely shoe shops earlier. Stuck proudly on the windows of Franco's small shop are photos of some of the happy ladies who have sat deferentially before him. They all look smug; some of them are famous. Cherie Blair smiles at Franco and ... yes ... there she is, all glossy, pouty lips and luscious boobies spilling out of a hot red dress—Liz Hurley. She was here just last week and the photo shows her sitting prettily, showing generous slices of bronzed cleavage while Franco fiddles at her feet. God, I'm impressed, as Franco intends me to be.

Dare I ask him if he has a sole big enough for me? Of course I bloody dare. He does, but he isn't about to give one to me without making me wait. He says he is too busy for me right now and I should come back in an hour. But when I do, he won't deign to attend to me and tells me to come back tomorrow. By this time I am obsessed. I must have some of his shoes, even if it means staying on Capri for the next ten years until he condescends to grant me a sitting.

I drag Geoffrey back the next day and am turned away again, but this time with a promise that Franco will attend me on my next visit. He does, after keeping me waiting for just half an hour. Finally, he leads me inside his shop, where he gets down two sets of his biggest soles from his stock of thousands and starts pulling out boxes of diamantés, gold and silver straps, black fringy things, pearly bits and gaudy strips of bright jewels. I am frightened of this man, much in the way I am of the Signora at the Villa Fabulous. I have no idea why, considering I am bigger than both of them and neither has really said or done anything rude to me. It's just that some people have an unmistakable air of authority, of cool disdain and I-can't-help-but-look-down-my-nose-at-you about them (or in my case, look up their nose, because I do stand taller than almost everyone else on earth).

So, because of my inferiority complex and fear of Franco, I gush on a bit and tell him he is a genius, a maestro of soles; he agrees completely and becomes almost friendly. He tells me he makes the soles on the Italian mainland every winter and sits outside his

Capri shop every summer fixing gorgeous bits onto the soles for fabulous and famous women—and in some cases people like me—and will I now please go away and come back again the next day?

So, what is this? Three, four or five visits for two pairs of flat sandals from Franco? I have lost count. Back I go again. Finally, Franco slips the finished products onto my feet like a reluctant prince who has had the rotten luck to cop the big ugly sister at the ball, and there I am with my handmade-just-for-me-drop-dead-gorgeous Italian sandals. One pair is a snakeskin number, the other a black-beaded beauty. I can't remember exactly how much they cost, but it did run into hundreds and Geoffrey recuperated quite well from his breakdown, thank you. And do you know what? To this day I have never worn those sandals. They simply will not stay on my feet. The thong bits won't stick between my toes and the snakeskin bits have small nails poking out of them. And even if I could get them to stay on, I couldn't walk in them; the soles are so slippery they skid across tiles and polished floors and refuse to grip onto pavements.

I could kill that Franco shyster. Not because his shoes are not fabulously glamorous—they are—but because he fooled me into thinking he was a shoe god. He was not. So, if you ever happen to be mingling with rich and famous people and find yourself on a red carpet somewhere and just happen to be behind Liz Hurley or Cherie Blair and see them stumbling and slipping about, don't be unkind and assume they've consumed one too many; blame that bastard Franco.

Fourteen

You might think we have been on Capri a long time … and you're right. We are staying on for another chapter, too, but don't fret, for soon I will take you to magnificent Rome and you're going to have the most fabulous time there, really.

Carlo, our waiter, concierge and factotum person at the Villa Fabulous, brings us our breakfast each morning. It is the same every day: sugary croissants, little hard rusk things similar to those we used to give our babies when they were teething, small packets of jam, tiny triangles of cream cheese and big cups of frothy milky coffee. Our breakfast is, of course, always offered with grace, style and many *prego*s.

We develop a little morning routine. We rise groggily, wash hastily, anxious to get out to the sunshine on the breakfast terrace, and quickly become addicted to the rusks and the cream cheese. We grow fond of Carlo and prefer to deal with him for our small needs rather than disturb the scary Signora. Once or twice we have required something when he is off duty and have had to draw on all our courage to approach her.

'Dare we most respectfully and obediently request a bottle of wine and two glasses from your small but lovely bar, if it isn't too inconvenient, and if it is we will gladly come back later', we grovel before her. But she is always pleasant and polite, if cool. I don't think she will ever forgive me for daring to doubt that her rooms were view-friendly.

Villa Fabulous, it must be said, is truly lovely. It is fairy small, maybe twelve rooms at the most, and wonderfully Italian. Obviously family-owned (we will never know for sure because we are too frightened to ask), it is spotless, stylish and spread over three levels. The breakfast terrace is unimaginably charming, its blue tiles reflecting the colour of the sky.

One morning as we sit with four other couples spaced around the terrace, Carlo appears a little nervous each time he approaches to refill our coffee. We sense he wants to say something, reveal some small secret perhaps, but is unsure of himself.

The other couples at Villa Fabulous at this time are all beautiful. Some Germans, plus an English pair of lovebirds—she a young slim sultry woman of great attractiveness who slinks on to the terrace each morning in a white sheath, he equally as gorgeous and slinky. We nod to them at breakfast but don't get into conversation. No-one wants to speak much in the mornings. The place is just too beautiful to waste with unnecessary words. Everyone sips, eats, crunches their rusks and stares out to the breathtaking scene.

As Carlo nervously approaches our table for perhaps the sixth time this morning, we sense he is finally about to spill out whatever is bothering him.

'*Scusi, Signora*', he says hesitantly, ever so politely, to me.

'Yes?' I ask encouragingly, because he is shaking a little and lightly perspiring.

'Are they yours?' he asks, screwing up his face with suppressed revulsion as he points to a tub of geraniums upon which, flapping happily, are my big knickers. They have fallen from our balcony above, where I had hung them to dry, and, as fate always dictates in ghastly situations such as this, they are my ugliest, rattiest, biggest pair. Actually, all my knickers are ugly, ratty and big, but these are just that bit more so.

I rush to the geranium pot, pick up the offending knickers and shove them up my sweater while Carlo slinks away, hunched over with embarrassment.

'You'll laugh about this one day', Geoffrey says helpfully.

We hire a small wooden boat at a cost that would have bought us a week of luxury on Hayman Island back in Australia, and plan a day sailing around the entire island. Capri is not a big island; to whiz around it quickly wouldn't take more than an hour, but we plan to stop and explore all the little coves and crannies.

After buying two huge sandwiches of ciabatta bread filled with bocconcini, tomatoes and basil, plus half a dozen bottles of water *and only one bottle of wine*, we point the boat in a clockwise direction around the island from Marina Piccola and head off in fine fettle.

Our little boat looks most humble as it chugs past some of the sleek yachts with beautiful people lazing about on the decks. But the front of ours has a little wooden platform thing with a padded mattress that I drape myself flabbily over and decide it is so comfortable that I don't give a toss what I look like.

We sail cautiously into a huge grotto then stop and anchor and jump into the deep blue water. I just can't describe to you how out-of-this-world good it is. After an hour we climb up the little ladder back into our boat and reluctantly sail out, continuing around the island. We crane our necks to look up at the cliffs and are amazed by the giant rocky structures and formations of chalky beauty, of slim lines and ridges in the rocks and fascinating caves and jutting-out bits that nature created thousands of years ago. We have our heads up most of the time, straining to capture it all, delighting in the seabirds swooping over the cliffs, the salty air, the lovely blue of the sea. We sail around to Anacapri, looking up to Hotel Caesar Augustus, which perches hundreds of metres above us on the cliffs and juts out precariously over the sea. We stop the boat for many minutes to look up in wonder, for it seems impossible that a vast and lavish hotel could be built so high up in the sky. We vow that one day we will save enough money to come back to Capri and stay a night, a week, a month at Hotel Caesar Augustus and experience life, even if just for a short while, on a five-star podium in the sky.

Eventually we come to *la Grotta Azzurra*, or, as we know it, the Blue Grotto. We have so far resisted all tours here, outraged at the ridiculously high cost to enter this famous grotto. It is one of the biggest tour operator rip-offs going on the island ... perhaps in the world. You pay three times to enter the grotto: first for the tour itself, then for a rower at the entrance in a small boat (because the large boats can't fit in), and then to actually enter.

'Wait until the tour boats leave at four every afternoon and you can swim in for free', we have been told and we—stingy, as we are— did try it one day, but the water was dangerously choppy and I had visions of being trapped by crashing waves blocking the small entrance and having to spend a lonely, wet night there until the tour boats came to my rescue in the morning. I had chickened out and now here we are outside the grotto, our little boat stopped with about thirty others. There is a flurry of noisy activity just outside the grotto as big tour boats discharge visitors into small rowing boats, necessary to get through the low, cave-like entrance. We yearn to go into the grotto and decide we have been too stingy on ourselves (and I still regret not paying to visit the Villa Jovis), so agree to pay and go inside. One of the operators says he will take us in for the equivalent of fifty dollars—yes, I can hardly believe it myself—and we anchor alongside him. With considerable effort, we get from our boat into his little boat and lie down flat as he ducks down and rows us inside. There are already at least ten other boats in here, crammed into the small-but-lofty space, but despite the crowd, it is just wondrous. The water is a blue so vivid it almost hurts our eyes, a luminous, incandescent blue cut by a thrilling, piercing shaft of brilliant sunlight coming through the small entrance and skimming the surface of the water. Our rower offers to wait a full two minutes if we want to jump off the boat and swim and, although we do want to very much, we decline, because we know if we jump into the water I will never get back into the boat again without the assistance of a ladder or perhaps a crane. So, our rower sings one line of 'O Sole Mio' and immediately rows us out again. Fifty dollars for three minutes and one line of a song. I am very annoyed that I haven't been able to indulge in the two-minute swim in the grotto; it is just too bad that middle age and a vast girth can often prevent you from taking full advantage of a situation.

We continue around the island in our little boat, sailing through the hole in the Faraglioni, stopping every now and again to swim in the clear water. I have written in my notes, 'Everyone should, even if it is just once, know the pleasure of swimming in this water, which can change from aquamarine to a deep inky colour within a few metres'. But this gushy little notation is followed by: 'Just as I was shouting and yelping with abandoned pleasure, there floated past me another armada of panty shields'. Charming!

But, back to food. We have some excellent meals on Capri. We pay big-time for them, but they are mostly unforgettable experiences, especially the long lunch at *Bagni di Tiberio* (the old baths of Tiberius). To get there we take the funicular down to the Marina Grande and then take the—wait for this—free boat around to the restaurant on the rocks. It is a Sunday and Bagni di Tiberio is very busy, packed with Italian families and big-breasted, bikini-topped beauties. There are very few tourists in the place, which gladdens our hearts (mine for the lack of tourists, Geoffrey's for the abundance of big-breasted, bikini-topped beauties).

Bagni di Tiberio specialises in seafood, which is evidenced by the big water tanks filled with live fish adorning the jetty leading to the restaurant's doors. We are the only couple at a table for two among big tables of eight, ten or twelve people, and indeed we appear to be the only tourists in a restaurant filled with large, lively, noisy families. It's perfect.

The *antipasti* bar to begin? Up we go to a long table filled with inviting dishes ... chargrilled peppers ... zucchini ... tiny rice-filled cherry tomatoes ... thin omelettes wrapped around bocconcini ... rolled slices of eggplant stuffed with pine nuts ... marinated fish ...

sliced potatoes … tomatoes filled with parmesan … spinach wrapped around pine nuts and olives. It is *so* good.

All around us the noise levels rise as families tuck into spaghetti and fresh fish, some passing big jugs of wine out to friends on the rocks outside the window. It is a scene of mild chaos and happy bedlam and couldn't be more Italian, and we are thrilled to be part of it.

We eat spaghetti with cherry tomatoes and those giant prawns that have heads the size of small lobsters. Next to us, a wrinkled old man sits importantly at the head of a table full of kids, teenagers and what are obviously extended family members, even a dog. They make enough noise for ten families, but it is wonderful noise that makes us happy and envious. Rarely do our own families get together in Australia (mine and Geoffrey's that is, not yours). Big space and small arguments separate us, and to watch close-knit Italian families gaining so much enjoyment from simply being at the same table can bring a lump to the throat.

One young boy at a big family table in front of us eats his way through a Mount Everest of spaghetti, followed by a huge plate of fried seafood, followed by an enormous slice of chocolate torte for dessert. I watch fascinated as he stuffs big forkfuls of spaghetti into his mouth and chomps and chomps, his little cheeks bulging with food, until the last strand is gone. His *nonna* sits at the head of his table, looking every bit the matriarch, except for the mobile phone stuck to her ear.

Our long meal over a leisurely afternoon is marvellous, perfect in fact, but when we finish and wander outside onto the rocks and discover another handkerchief of free beach, we feel completely fulfilled. We squeeze in between an attractive young mother breast-feeding her baby and a dozing man of vast fatness, sit down and promptly fall asleep—as you do when you are full of good food, excellent wine and complete contentment.

Another long lunch that sticks (hazily) in our memory takes place at Le Grotelle, near L'Arco Naturale. In a setting so remarkable it makes us giggle stupidly in disbelief that we are really here—we are perched on a terrace so high that we actually look down on tree tops and swooping seagulls; the kitchen is carved into the cliff wall and the tables and chairs perch very close to the cliff's edge—we eat freshly chargrilled vegetables and delicious ravioli. We hold great hope for the fish dish to follow—the restaurant's specialty—but what actually comes is two tiny blobs of plain fish. What the fish lacks in taste, however, the house wine makes up for in fruity style. It is so good we have three bottles. I have written **THREE BOTTLES** in capital letters in my diary notes, which proves that I sometimes even shock myself. I like to think our indulgence is only because we cannot tear ourselves away from the view and not because we are hopeless drunks.

Here's another diary note from Capri:

We walked down the Via Krupp after jumping over the fence. I am quite used to the fence now, and leap over it like a goat. Actually, I feel like a goat, or rather a pig. I am sunburnt, covered in sandfly bites and have broken out in sun blisters on my lips, which are turning into cold sores. I am scratched all down my arms from scrambling down to the rocks to swim, I have rolls of fat around my middle and I feel absolutely revolting.

While I certainly remember feeling fat in Italy, I don't recall being sunburnt or bitten by a single sandfly. It's funny how time gives us rose-coloured memories, and just as well we do have selective memories, because even on an idyllic island surrounded by loveliness, I can manage to feel like a slob.

We enjoy another memorable lunch in a restaurant on Marina Piccola, right on the water's edge overlooking the beach. Watching the children play on the pebbled beach and frolic in the water while we eat fresh melon and prosciutto is charming, but it is the waiter who captures my attention. Harried and flustered, he reminds me of Manuel from *Fawlty Towers*. He appears to be looking after the busy floor himself and is having trouble taking the many orders. His inner Manuel leaps out in a big way when a group of young American men come in and start ordering in rapid English as though they are in a Sizzler in Seattle.

'Does that ravioli have cheese on it and is it parmesan, 'cos if it is I don't want it, I want the lasagna, but only if it has chunky meat in it, not that crappy ground beef but proper meat, and can I have a salad on the side, fat-free mayo of course, heavy on the tomatoes and hold the onions. And gimmie a Sprite with ice. Actually, better make that a Diet Coke. No, on second thoughts, I'll have an iced tea.'

They say all of this without actually looking at the menu or the waiter, let alone first inquiring 'Do you speak English?', then become annoyed when Manuel shakes his head in confusion, shrugs his shoulders and runs away.

Our best discovery is Ristorante Pizzeria da Gemma, down a narrow street off Piazza Umberto I and through the steps of the lovely church that we still haven't looked in. It is a big restaurant packed with tables overlooking Marina Grande, and has a generous and colourful *antipasti* bar in its centre. We fill up on chargrilled vegetables and marinated fish and oily octopus and spinach stuffed with pine nuts. We should and could stop at this because we are so full, but we go on to Gemma's special spaghetti with those delicious tiny cherry tomatoes and basil. This is one of the best places to watch the early evening slowly grow to darkness. We look down to the hills as they come alive with twinkling lights and then up to the sky, and it appears as though we are suspended in a vast landscape where stars are both above and beneath us.

After the experience of our first dangerous walk to Anacapri, we decide to take the bus for further visits, and upon doing so we encounter more thrills. We are shunted with the crowds onto the bus through a series of iron walkways, then herded towards the back by urgent shouts from the driver. Only a fortunate few get a seat and when we are pushed and compressed as much as possible into this moving sardine can, twenty more people squeeze on.

On any normal day I could not bear to have a fat man's belly pressed into my back, nor a fleshy breast nestled under my arm, nor various other body parts mashed intimately against me, but today there is no room for propriety, particularly as my own ample protuberances are indelicately shoved in a skinny man's (the only one on the bus) face.

Once the bus is frighteningly full, it clatters off, only to stop about 300 metres up the road to let on another ten people with bulging shopping bags. Up the hazardous road we chug, clinging tightly to the hanging straps and hoping everyone is wearing deodorant, swaying as one big body as the driver blasts his horn and navigates the treacherous hairpin bends. Around the frightening curves we go, almost scraping the small iron fence separating the bus from the terrifying drop several hundred metres below. I begin to pray. 'Please, don't let all the fat people lean forward at this moment to peer down at the spectacular view, because we will certainly topple over the cliffs, and I have always hoped for a clean, swift death, not a messy one involving me being dashed to pieces on rocks. And if you answer my prayers I'll give up drinking forever.'

We do make it around the bend, and as the bus driver changes gear in anticipation of another tight corner and as everyone's sweaty flesh presses together again, someone squeezes his hand down, fumbles in a pocket, pulls out a packet of cigarettes and lights up.

I know you think I exaggerate, but really, truly, honestly and sincerely, I don't.

Capri grows more beautiful as our time here runs out. We know we will not be able to afford to come back for a long, long time, possibly never. This is reinforced to us late one night, after one of those stomach-swelling dinners at Gemma's. We have been told of a nightclub that is so lively we absolutely must experience it, even if it is just once. People sing and clap to rousing music and get so carried away that they jump from the floor up onto the table in one energetic leap. (You try doing that without the assistance of a trampoline.) It sounds typical of the way Italians go about enjoying themselves, and we just have to experience it.

We force ourselves to stay awake, because the action doesn't start until midnight and most nights we are passed out in a food-wine-and-Limoncello coma before ten. Like all really good nightspots, this one is down a dark alley and very difficult to find, but after stumbling around and stubbing toes and bumping knees for half an hour, we finally come across it. Two handsome young men at the door welcome us in and ask us for the equivalent of a hundred dollars. Just to get in! We hand them the money and are about to go in when the shock hits us. How can we pay a hundred dollars just to enter a place? We ask for our money back and leave, hugely distressed to think we have almost parted with a vast amount of cash just to see someone jump up onto a table.

We go back to Villa Fabulous, sit on our balcony and open another bottle of Limoncello to console ourselves. As we are nodding off half an hour later—dribbling lightly, no doubt—one of the glamorous yachts anchored below us puts on a fifteen-minute fireworks display from its decks. Now this is exciting.

The noise reverberates across the bay and up onto the cliffs. Dogs bark in protest, cats howl in tune and people leap from their beds to witness the brilliant display. It is like New Year's Eve 2000 in Sydney, and all from the deck of a boat. And to think, if we'd paid a hundred dollars to go into that nightclub to watch someone jump up onto a table, we would have missed it.

Fifteen

I hope I have not given you the very wrong impression that Geoffrey and I have a drinking problem. It's just that when we are on holiday we tend to get into the bottle a lot more than usual. At home our eating and drinking routine is simple, Spartan almost. We never get properly stuck into the wine until the weekend, we try to get through our eight glasses of water each day and eat at least five serves of vegetables and three of fruit, and we even embrace brown rice and tofu occasionally. But take us on a holiday or send us away for a naughty weekend and we go berserk.

Let me take you back to Australia for a brief time, where our habits and culture differ so strongly from those in Italy. Our over-indulgence is never more evident than at breakfast buffets in hotels. While at home during the course of a busy week, deep into our routines, we can happily start our mornings with a bowl of All-Bran and prunes and a tub of fat-free yogurt, put us in a hotel breakfast buffet line and weird things happen. We sprint past the cereal in our rush to get to the hash browns, sneer at the fruit on our run to the bacon, almost spit in the bowl of prunes on our jog to the sausages, then scoff at the fat-free yogurts as we race to the fried egg section. Geoffrey has been known to take four fried eggs at once and I, if I am to be perfectly honest, have been caught slipping an extra sausage onto a plate already over-flowing with three greasy hash browns, two rashers of crispy bacon, a big puddle of baked beans and a couple of cholesterol-ridden eggs benedict. This is why I take only Lycra waist-expanding clothes on holiday. It is also one of the reasons I like Italy; very few places there serve the big, artery-clogging breakfasts. They stick to the sugary stuff.

It's not just the breakfast buffet that brings out the beast in me; I cannot restrain myself at the buffet at any time of day. Put me in front of the seafood stand and I get a bit silly. Don't you tut-tut at me, I am not alone in my buffet greed. I have watched plenty of people elbow their way into the prawns and calamari, pile their plates dangerously high and then top it all off with a huge slice of pavlova and a dollop of chocolate mousse. Admit it: most of us become people possessed at the buffet. I mean, really, in a normal à la carte situation, would you order your prawns on the same plate as your pavlova? Of course you wouldn't, but the race to fill your plate with as much food as possible before some other greedy oaf nicks all the prawns or takes the last bit of pavlova is difficult to resist, isn't it?

Most Australians I know love a buffet. I was once at a lunchtime wine festival where winemakers offered tastings of thousands of bottles of wine for an all-inclusive-one-off-payment. Chefs manned food stalls all around the area and cooked sumptuous morsels to go with the wine all afternoon. As the day wore on it became quite a competition to see how much all-included-in-the-price grog and food could be thrown down throats. By four in the afternoon, every drop of wine was gone and there was a panicky stampede on the sherry stand. All afternoon the poor sherry representative had tried to give away tastes of his product and been rudely ignored, but he now found himself buried alive beneath six hundred drunks. They actually knocked the stand over in their greedy haste, but if we were to talk to these people in the sober light of the next day, they would tell us they barely drink. It's the line-up-and-take-all-you-can-get syndrome that makes us so greedy, and we all fall into it. Except you, of course.

Fortunately, Italians do not go for the buffet at many places.

When Italians find out we are Australian (not German), they become very friendly. They seem to love Aussies, and almost every one of them has a cousin, uncle or brother in Australia. Most Italians we meet say they yearn to visit Australia but probably never will. It's simply too far away and the long flight is too daunting.

Like most people who have never been to Australia, many Italians really do think we have kangaroos hopping down our city streets and living in our backyards. Very few people believe me when I tell them that most Australians only see kangaroos in sanctuaries or on trips to the country. Foreigners seem to think of us living in Australia with deadly snakes slithering into our lounge rooms on a nightly basis, poisonous spiders nesting under our pillows and curious goannas appearing at our back doors at dinner-time. But, to be fair, in some parts of Australia this is almost the case. I experienced this myself once, way up in the steamy north one hot wet February a few years ago. My daughter who lives up there had been struck down with Dengue Fever and I had gone to her bedside. She was living as only the young can, in a house with about twenty other itinerate young people, and her bedroom was best described as a cave with a dirt floor dug into the side of a crumbling old house. Her cave door was a loose bit of that green netting shadecloth you use in the garden and was all that stood between her and a neglected algae-ridden swimming pool in the back yard. The pool was the perfect home for Dengue mosquitoes, so it was only natural that she would one day be bitten. Anyway, she became very sick and I became very distraught, so I flew to her bed-side and took my beautiful young daughter out of her sweltering cave and into an air-conditioned hotel room. There she lay in a big bed with clean sheets while I sat and watched her waste away before my weeping eyes for a whole week while torrential rain roared and gushed outside day and night. There was nothing we could do but let the fever take its course. The doctor visited every day to take blood from her withering arms for tests and I held up her aching head so she could take regular sips of water. Apart from that, she just slept and slept and got weaker and weaker. But after six days the fever abated and she could sit up; on the seventh day she could get up and I am happy to report that she made a full and complete recovery and is once again a lovely voluptuous young woman. And she no longer lives in a cave. But it was a terrible, awful week, and people do die from Dengue Fever.

On the last day, when I knew she was going to be okay, I took some friends who live there out for dinner. I called a taxi and on the way to dinner the driver regaled me with a gruesome story about an American tourist he had just taken to hospital. She had been stupid enough to step into the sea at that time of year and had been stung by a jellyfish-stinger-thing.

'Her leg looked as though someone had taken a blowtorch to it', he told me gleefully. 'There are signs up everywhere telling people not to go into the water. I can't think how she could have been so stupid. God, you should have seen the sting on her leg, it looked like a terrible burn.'

So, here we have a young woman almost dying from a mosquito bite and another with a wound like a blowtorch burn inflicted by a small jellyfish. I discussed this with my friends over dinner and they reassured me that it was safe to live with these creatures if you knew how to avoid them.

At the end of dinner I called a taxi and was driven once again by the gruesomely gleeful taxi driver. 'Sorry I'm a bit late', he said. 'I was held up by a monstrous python sleeping in the middle of the road and I had to wait until someone came and prodded him and he moved on.'

On another visit to our daughter, who was living in yet another horrible shared house, we saw giant ants crawling all over her messy kitchen. These fellows were so huge that two of them could lift a pappadum that had been left on the table from the previous night's curry takeaway. We walked into the kitchen and saw what appeared at first glance to be a pappadum walking up the wall by itself, but on closer inspection turned out to be a pappadum being happily carried up the wall by a couple of Arnie Schwarzenegger-styled ants. How impressive is that?

This is all true. Mosquitoes that can kill, jellyfish that burn, giant pythons that stop traffic and ants that can lift pappadums.

In steamy northern parts of Australia, you expect creepy crawlies and slithering things, but try telling foreigners that most Australians live in highly developed areas where the chance of seeing an unpleasant creature is quite small.

I remember an English cousin from London visiting my mother in Melbourne for the first time a few years ago. Despite my telling her what a cosmopolitan and vibrant city Melbourne is, she still telephoned me in Queensland soon after her arrival to say how surprised she was to find that all the men didn't walk around wearing hats with corks bobbing from the rims. The awful thing about this is that she wasn't being sarcastic, she was quite sincere.

A friend recently sent me an email with extracts from letters of would-be immigrants written to the Department of Immigration. I promise you these are real questions.

I hear that Australian women are beautiful. Is that true and if so, can you send me pictures of the available ones? This came from Italy, of course.

Can I wear high heels in Australia? This came from the UK. (It could quite possibly have been a friend of my cousin.)

Do you have perfume in Australia? From France.

Are there places in Australia where you can make love outdoors? No prizes for guessing where this came from.

Can I drive to the Great Barrier Reef? The Germans.

Can you tell me the regions in Tasmania where the female population is larger than the male population? Yet another question from a horny Italian.

Will I be able to speak English most places I go? This beauty came from the US.

Can you give me some information on hippo racing in Australia?

Me rushing to the buffet table is about the only hippo racing I know of in Australia.

Sixteen

I will start this chapter on Rome by telling you a naughty story, so if you don't like smut, skip on a bit. It's time for a bit of sex anyway; we haven't had any since the Italian gigolos in the first chapter.

In 1966, during that first trip back to England, I teamed up with another big strapping Aussie girl and we bought an old Bedford van that was barely roadworthy, threw a mattress in the back and rattled off to do Europe for four months. The van constantly broke down but we always found a bunch of young men willing to tow us to the nearest garage or fix the problem for us. God, I can imagine myself at the side of a road now with my emergency lights flashing: I'd be left there until the end of time. But back then, however, we had only to jump out of the van, lift the hood, bend over the engine and a crowd of men would appear from the bushes, brandishing big tyre levers and offering mechanical advice and lewd propositions. We took the advice and assistance, rejected the

propositions and tootled off without a care for thousands of kilometres around Europe in an unsafe vehicle. As you do when you
are young.

The van was too clumsy to park in the centre of big cities, so we
would head for a camping ground outside town, settle into a spot
for a few days and then hitchhike into city centres and do all the
sightseeing stuff and look for suitable suitors. Hitchhiking was
so very easy and we never had to wait more than a mini-second,
due the mini-ness of our skirts. Our willing unpaid taxi drivers
always delivered us to wherever we wanted to go and when it was
time to go home there was always another line-up of men to drive
us back. (If my two lovely twenty-something daughters are reading
this now—DON'T YOU DARE HITCHHIKE. EVER. DO YOU
HEAR ME?)

This sounds trite, but it really was safe back then. We never felt
threatened. Except once—well, maybe not threatened, unless you
call keeling over and choking with laughter a threat. After we had
settled into our camp several kilometres outside Rome, we squeezed
into our miniskirts, stuck on our fake hairpieces, plastered our eyes
with blue eye shadow and our lips with pale shimmering lipstick
and set off to do the town. A small owlish man in a tiny Fiat stopped
for us the second we stood at the roadside. His English was limited,
but it was easy to make him understand we wanted to go right into
Rome, to be dropped off at the Colosseum, thank you, as close as
possible, if you don't mind. Then we sat back and completely
ignored him. Our rudeness, looking back thirty-eight years later,
makes me blush with guilt and remorse. I sat in the front with my
long legs scrunched floppily up to my bosoms and chatted over my
shoulder to my friend squeezed into the back, never once looking at
our driver. When we had almost reached our destination our man

stopped the car on the busy road and indicated that he was going to attend to something in the engine, which was in the back, as you people who know about Fiats would know. Cars piled up behind and crawled around us, horns tooted, shouts came from windows, but still I sat chatting over my shoulder to my friend, ignoring the little man, waiting for him to fix the engine and to deliver us to the very front of the Colosseum. Then something made me look back. There was our man, peering lustily at us through a slit in the hood, masturbating furiously. In the centre of Rome. In the street. In the open air. Alfresco pudding-pulling.

It wasn't so much his blatant disregard for propriety or his fast hand action that shocked me, it was more our rudeness in ignoring him, at not realising that having two voluptuous Australian girls in his car had made him very horny, baby.

Like young women do when they receive a small shock of the sexual kind, we shrieked girlishly and tried to leap out of the tiny car, which wasn't easy, because we were really quite big and the car was so very small. Our man did not miss a beat and continued his frantic activity. He was, if I can convince you to believe me, a gentleman. I say this confidently, because he came around to the car door to us and with his free hand and some pleading words indicated that if we were willing to wait—it wouldn't take much longer—he would be quite happy to drive us on to our destination. We declined.

This little incident could go a long way to explain my affection for Italian men; when the need grips, so do they, no matter where they may be. I am not suggesting for a single moment that all, or even a few, of those gorgeous Italian men go about this usually private activity in alfresco circumstances, but in this instance one did, and it really was very funny at the time.

Men are the same all over the world. What is it about their willies that so fascinates them? From the moment they are old enough to work their arms and can reach down and touch their little things, they rarely leave them alone. A couple of enterprising Australian guys have turned their willie-fiddling into a money-making enterprise and now tour the world doing a show called 'Puppetry of the Penis' in which they stand on stage for a full hour completely naked, pulling and stretching their genitalia into the kind of shapes you never thought could be possible from a meaty lump and some wrinkly skin. Now, don't you dare tell me you're not madly impressed. What started out as tricks at the pub—you know the sort of sporty thing, where a bloke sticks that little wire bit off the champagne cork over the end of his penis to a hearty round of applause from his mates—has turned into a crowd-drawing show.

I was coerced into attending their show by a dozen female friends who probably thought it a good idea to have a token older woman in the group for safety. We had the bad luck to be sitting in the front row, which terrified me at first because the words 'audience' and 'participation' had been bandied around and I was sitting right in front of the steps leading down from the stage. There were nine hundred people behind me (yes, I find it difficult to believe nine hundred people actually paid good money to see two blokes playing with their crown jewels too) and I was the most obvious 'audience participator' in the vast auditorium. Can you imagine my relief when a rowdy group of drunk hens' night girls, complete with penis-shaped name tags and a bride-to-be in a fluoro pink veil with flashing fairy lights, made its raucous way into the auditorium to take up the rest of the front row? The bride had 'audience participator and big-time sucker' written all over her sloshed face.

There was much build-up to the puppeteers' entry. Music, drum-rolls, dramatic announcements, no-photographs-please warnings and mist wafting over the stage … and finally, there they were. Two good-looking young men in full-length capes, which were shed after a brief introduction.

Confrontingly naked apart from sneakers, they literally cranked the show up, winding their penises like organ grinders, stretching and turning until the entire audience gasped in vicarious pain. And that was just the start of the pulling, stretching, kneading, squeezing, contorting, rolling, extending, yanking, pushing, con-tracting, manipulating, bending and shaping that went on for the next hour.

We were shown how to make a brain (how appropriate) from a tightly squeezed testicle, a windsurfer's sail from a scrotum, a turtle from a squashed-in penis and a didgeridoo from a stretched-out one, as well as a hamburger from the entire genitalia package. There was just so much to learn, and all from my close-up bird's-eye position below the stage.

And don't you worry about those people up the back. A camera-woman captured it all in full, stretchy close-up and beamed it onto a giant screen behind the naked men. These guys certainly had their fingers on the pulse when it came to knowing their audience; without pausing, they kept the dick tricks going non-stop until the dreaded audience participation part. For this they made the bride-to-be stand on stage and hold her hands out wide as though she was describing a recently caught large fish. Then one of them, pretending to be a fruit bat, ran jigglingly around the stage before doing a perfect handstand in front of her. His legs were spread to the width of her arms and she had no choice but to hold them. With her nose just centimetres from his hanging fruit bat and her fluoro headgear flashing brightly, it made for the perfect wedding album photo.

The puppeteers then went on to shape their genitals into Uluru (at sunset—they really turned purple), hungry pelicans, hot dogs, Kentucky Fried Chicken (I'll never touch it again), Olympic torches, the Eiffel Tower, a bulldog ... I could go on forever. But I'd better not. I think I should take you back to Rome in more genteel circumstances, with Geoffrey in 2000, where we can afford a bit of comfort and the likelihood of coming across an alfresco masturbator is small.

Rome—and all the grime and flurry associated with any big city— is not easy on the eyes after Capri. After a wistful goodbye to the lovely island and a polite farewell to the Signora who, now that we were leaving, seemed very agreeable, happy almost, we endured a packed ferry from Capri then enjoyed a comfortable, efficient train from Naples.

Our hotel on Via Quattro Fontane in Rome is not good. 'Located in an old palace built in the eighteenth century', it sounded promising in the brochure, but 'specialising in looking after bus groups' should have warned us. A huge crowd of middle-aged and elderly American and German tourists in garishly checked bermuda shorts and floral capri pants with those hideous bumbags around their thick waists pushes its way into the lobby with suitcases and backpacks, shouting and screeching at each other. It takes us many minutes to manoeuvre through and around them to the reception desk, where a man looks at us as though we have just arrived, not from the gorgeous island of Capri, but from a leper colony. He speaks a few supercilious English words to us, hands us a key and a map and points to the lift.

We of course have the worst room in the hotel, down the end of a corridor lined with dull carpet and smelling of must dating back to the eighteenth century. Stifling and claustrophobia-inducing, our room has only one small window, high up on the wall overlooking a wide, leafy street and the windows of a neighbouring hotel. The room puts us in a filthy mood. We trip over and bump into each other while trying to unpack in the few square centimetres of space between the bed and the wardrobe.

'Let's go out and look around', I say, to keep us from ripping each other's eyes out.

It is late afternoon, oppressively hot and many of the shops are still closed for siesta, which doesn't improve our mood. Our hotel, while being ultra crappy, does enjoy a marvellous location very close to the Trevi Fountain, the Spanish Steps and Via Veneto. We head first for the Trevi Fountain, to recapture the romance we shared there thirty-five years ago. We clamber past the giant tour buses outside the square and pick our way politely through the squillion people clogged around the fountain. After getting nowhere, we begin to gently push to try and get through the mob, but our courteous *scusi*s soon turn to irritated *do you mind*s and before long to *get out of my way, you selfish brute*s as we elbow and shove just like everyone else to get close to the fountain.

This is the ugly side of tourism. We hate it but can't avoid it if we like to visit Italy in the summer, which we do, because what is the use of a tourist-free winter visit when all the museums and galleries and restaurants are closed? But these crowds, especially in the heat, can cause the most patient person to lose her temper and the most polite person to become one of the ugly crowd she despises.

We finally manage to get a seat on the ledge of the fountain and try to think back to our honeymoon years, when we had this magnificent place to ourselves. It simply doesn't work; the chaos kills any chance of romance. Our attempts to take a photo of each other with the fountain backdrop of Neptune, God of the Sea, almost result in a fistfight. The clogged and crowded atmosphere makes it impossible for me to take a photo of Geoffrey on his own, so we give up on this idea and try for a picture of him sitting on the fountain ledge with a bunch of unattractive strangers, but every time I quickly line the shot up, someone walks right in front of the camera. I do, however, manage a good one of him with a huge pair of breasts in his face and he snaps one of me with my face screwed up in anger, silently shouting an obscenity at a passerby. We take similar photos of ourselves standing on the Spanish Steps. You cannot tell we are actually standing on the steps, because there are about a zillion other people with us, but if you look closely, through the crowd standing, lying, resting, sitting, sleeping and half-dozing, you can spot Geoffrey's right shoe.

We abandon the fountain and romantic memories and wander off to find Via Veneto, Rome's most fashionable street. Celebrity spotting on Via Veneto is almost guaranteed, according to a glossy brochure we find in our hotel lobby. Absolutely anyone who is famous goes there, including Liz Hurley—she especially loves Harry's Bar, as does Hugh Grant (but not with her) and Sylvester Stallone. Right now, so do Ann and Geoffrey Rickard.

We sit inside Harry's in richly upholstered chairs admiring the dark panelled walls and thick velvet curtains, me looking a good year younger and a few kilos slimmer (I like to think) in the shadowy glow from small red lamps.

Elegant waiters in formal suits glide regally around the floor. It all makes Geoffrey decidedly nervous, because although a drink only is our intention, we know the bill will send us whimpering and snivelling into the hot streets.

Our gin-and-tonics are served with a silver bowl of peanuts complete with a silver spoon to dish them out. Same peanuts, grander presentation, even more pride. I spot a sexy woman falling out of a tight red dress drinking a martini in a corner with a distinguished-looking silver-haired man. I just know she is Liz. But during a trip to the ladies for a closer inspection, Liz turns out to be an older woman, fattish, big boobies bursting down her front, thick layers of make-up, no pouty lips. It is obvious that there will be no celebrity spottings in Harry's tonight, but we are well compensated by the nibblies. As well as peanuts, we are served hot canapés. They look fantastic on their little silver dish, but turn out to be nothing more than warmed-up focaccias cut into little squares, one with cheese, one with salami. But who cares, it's Harry's Bar and these little nibblies are well worth the sixty-five dollar bill that comes with them and the two gin-and-tonics.

Harry's Bar also has a restaurant, which we check out before leaving. It looks a bit like I imagine the dining room at Buckingham Palace to look like: over-the-top extravagance, with an ornate fireplace in the centre of the room and immaculate linen-topped tables set with polished silverware and gold-rimmed maroon plates. It is still early and the place is empty but for a fabulous-looking maître d wiping imaginary marks off the big sparkling glasses, checking out the spotless silver and issuing urgent instructions to a team of minions. The scene terrifies Geoffrey, so we wander back down Via Veneto to find many of the restaurants now doing a brisk trade, their waiters outside spruiking for customers.

We choose the one with the most tables on the footpath, then order a pizza with four cheeses and a pasta with tomato sauce and a jug of house wine; boring, but that's all there is. We are enjoying the mediocre food and lazy action of the street and trying our hardest to ignore all the Americans around us ordering Sprite with ice, when something hard and vibrating is thrust into my back. On certain occasions—and I can't think of one right now—this would not be entirely unwelcome, but memories of 1966 and my masturbatory chauffeur are strong in my mind, so I turn angrily to find a gypsy massaging my back with a vibrating hairbrush. She urges me to buy this ridiculous thing and I almost do, but there is something about her runny nose and lack of teeth, not to mention Geoffrey's worried rummaging in his wallet, that turns me off. The moment I reject her, another takes her place selling something crappy, then another selling flawless long-stemmed red roses and then another—my absolute favourite—selling small statues of David that are actually cigarette lighters. This particular gypsy thrusts it at my face, babbling something incoherent and when I push it away, she shoves it back again, this time flicking the top of David's head whereupon his penis lights up with a little spurt and a small flame. It is so good I want to take up smoking, I want to buy a caseload of them. But of course I don't. And I deeply regret this now, because it is all too rare that a penis lights up for me these days.

Gypsies are a nuisance all over Rome. They don't particularly bother me, but they do scare me a little, especially the old crones who sit like crumpled piles of dirty blankets on the footpaths outside every tourist spot, shaking uncontrollably, rattling tins and crying out beseechingly. There is something decidedly uncanny about them, apart from the obvious. We don't realise what it is until Charlie and Eva—well experienced in the habits of gypsies ever since one stole Charlie's wallet from deep within his front pocket over which he had his hand protectively at the time—tell us that these gypsies are actually young, beautiful, strong women with hot bodies camouflaged by the old rags and filthy scarves covering most of their face. This seems a bit stupid to me, because if I was a young, beautiful, strong woman with a hot body, I could think of better ways to earn a living than sitting on hard concrete outside the Sistine Chapel pretending to be an old woman in stinking rags, shaking like a leaf and begging for money.

And why do these gypsies always come at you when you are doing something self-indulgent like eating in an overpriced restaurant or drinking at a footpath café? One did it to us in Santa Margherita as we were enjoying our usual *aperitivo* or six at an especially delightful café with tables and chairs that took up almost the width of a back-street. A dreadful slobbering woman approached us, one arm holding a baby that looked as though it had been given a quarter bottle of Valium, the other outstretched, pleading for money. She wailed some kind of mantra at us over and over again, pointing to her baby. Her desperation had me reaching for my purse until a waiter told me not to be ridiculous, she was a regular at this café at this time of evening. She was after a vodka martini. With a lemon twist, please.

The gypsy I most admire is a good-looking pre-pubescent boy at the top of the Spanish Steps who thrusts a single white rose at me from a long big bunch and says, 'I give you, I give you, I give you'. I reject him immediately, because I believe that gypsies do not give you anything unless it is some disease of the kind you can't bring yourself to tell your mother about. But he persists.

'No money, no money', he says. 'I give you, I give you.' He presses the rose onto me, his face a picture of innocence, his gesture saying, 'I am giving a *bella donna* a white rose because I have spotted her in the crowd and am so taken by her style and elegance and fabulous presence only a beautiful single rose will do for her'. I'm tempted.

'I don't want it, really, I don't', I say and make my way down another few steps over strewn and sitting bodies.

'You must take it', he says and thrusts it again at me until I have no choice but to take it. The little blighter then immediately takes off, makes his hasty way down to the bottom of the steps, leaping over the crowds and accidentally kicking a few heads, to meet me at the bottom with a look of such pleading and his hand outstretched that I would gladly give him a hundred dollars for his bloody rose.

Of course I don't. I give him a hundred lire instead, which instantly wipes the imploring look off his face and brings forth a snort of disgust and a stream of well-aimed spit at my lovely rose. Serves me right for believing in gypsies bearing gifts. And for being so stingy. How much is a hundred lire, anyway? About ten cents?

Our breakfast in the morning is definitely the low point of our time in Italy. Every middle-aged and doddering tourist in the hotel has decided to breakfast at once in the too-small dining area. The Americans push the Germans, the English shove the Americans and everyone battles for a spot at the too-few tables. Miserable-looking croissants, hard bread and something masquerading as jam sit on a buffet table and are fought over energetically as though they are gourmet fare.

Some of the tourists fill up little thermoses with hot water from the urn and pinch tea bags and sachets of coffee, obviously to consume later on the bus. This bothers me a lot. No matter how old or infirm I become (actually, I am almost there), I will never take one of these big bus tours, I will never succumb to pinching a tea bag and a bit of hot water.

And no matter how bad the food is in any place, I will never complain to the waiter. You might snort and call me a hypocrite, but if you had once interviewed a slightly inebriated chef (he had to be, otherwise he never would have revealed his dirty little secret) who told you that he would flop his penis out onto the plate of any customer who made a fuss, you would never complain again either. This unsavoury little story is true, I promise. Another ghastly one I heard, which could well be made up, came from a group of flight attendants, who told me that if a passenger was particularly offensive, they would take the meat, fish or chicken part of his meal, give it a good swish around the toilet bowl before putting it back on his plate, then one by one go and stand by his seat to inquire, ever so politely, 'How is your meal, sir? To your liking?'. These same flight attendants warned me to always lock up my toothbrush in hotels in countries inhabited by people who dislike Americans/Australians/ the English—and isn't that just about every country these days?— because the housekeeping staff will use it to clean the toilet and then put it back where you left it.

How on earth did I get onto that subject?

We join the several million other tourists in the blazing sun outside St Peter's Basilica to queue in a long zigzag sheep-pen-thing and slowly wind our way to the entrance. Everywhere, tour group leaders guide their members by holding up sticks tied with hats or scarves or, in one case, a big yellow bumblebee. Some of the tour leaders choose to have all their members wear the same swamp-green hats or puke-yellow scarves around their necks, in boy scout style. A whole bunch of old people wearing matching boy scout scarves looks only marginally more ridiculous than a whole bunch of people following a bumblebee, in my opinion. But I shouldn't judge. No matter how ancient or dementia-ridden I become (actually, I am nearly there too) I will never join a tour and be led around by a bumblebee.

I remember coming here in 1966, when the queues were tiny and getting into St Peter's was quick and easy except for a man on duty at the door. His job was to check out the legs of every woman coming through—goodness knows how much training he had to do or how many thousands of other applicants he had to beat to get such an enviable position. Knees were unseemly inside St Peter's, which meant that very few females at the time were permitted in, especially me in my skirt that more closely resembled a belt. The leg policeman was furious with me and my tiny skirt and ordered me away from the steps even before I got a look in. I remember my acute disappointment, but there was no point in going back for another skirt, because they all looked like belts.

But now, in 2000, we have been warned against shorts and told that shoulders must be covered, so we are prepared. By the time the queue has shuffled its way to the door, everyone in it is very distressed by the heat. Women are fanning themselves with magazines, men are dabbing their brows with handkerchiefs and clothes are stuck to perspiring bodies. I think that, like me, everyone is wondering if this long wait is going to be worth it. So imagine our relief on stepping inside the vast coolness of St Peter's; it is like climbing up a long, hot ladder from the heat of hell and stepping into cool marble heaven.

If breakfast this morning was a low point of the trip, then this is a high. The space. The wealth. The statues. The sculptures. The height. So immense and lofty is this space that once the hordes of tourists are inside and split up, they look like clusters of ants. It is all simply too much to take in, so for half an hour we just wander, mouths open, looking up at some of the marble statues, incredulous at the detail. We take many photos: me standing dwarfed by a sculpture of a woman holding a baby, the marble folds of her robe falling as softly as silk ... me standing by a square column so wide that twenty more people could stand beside me and we would still not cover its width ... me standing metres beneath a couple of marble angels playing flutes. We look up to wonder after wonder and I take back every scornful thing I said about not wanting to belong to a tour group with a bumblebee leader, because right now I want a knowledgeable person to tell me everything about every piece of magnificent art in this amazing place.

We do sneak up to several groups to eavesdrop, but only catch snippets before some observant person notices we aren't wearing a puke-yellow scarf or swamp-green hat and glares at us until we slope guiltily off. We spend an hour in the cool hallowed space, marvelling at the acres of gold, mountains of marble and rows of huge paintings, wondering how many massive teams of people it must have taken to do all this.

The trouble with so much splendour in one place is that you can easily become blasé. When there is too much to marvel at, wayward thoughts creep into your minds ... 'Yeah, so here's another incredible statue, but God, I'd kill for a pizza' ... 'Fabulous painting, but really, there's another one over there and I am starving now'. Horrified by these heretical thoughts, we join another group to eavesdrop, where we learn that Michelangelo designed St Peter's and Giovanni Lorenzo Bernini created the *piazza*. The square was constructed between 1506 and 1626, an unimaginable effort when you consider they didn't have a single Black & Decker back then. Thousands of people can be accommodated in the square. Perhaps the most famous treasure among all the marble and gold is Michelangelo's *Pietà*.

Fair enough, but I want a pizza.

Seventeen

Città del Vaticano—the Vatican City—is the smallest independent state in Europe, located in Rome with a population of fewer than a thousand. I know this because it is written in my diary and I must have copied it from a guidebook. You, however, probably already knew it.

The Vatican City includes the Vatican Museums, the Sistine Chapel, the Vatican Gardens, St Peter's Basilica, St Peter's Square, the Vatican post office and the tourist centre. It is located on the west bank of the river Tevere and is separated from the rest of Rome by a wall. I bet you knew that too.

Geoffrey and I walk along this wall, into the Sistine Chapel. This is another place that overwhelms us with grandeur but has us thinking of pizza after half an hour. It is simply too much to take in. The tapestries, the gold, the paintings, the sculptures, the statues, the 'ancient urns and stuff' (as I write in my diary) and the ceiling are grandeur on a scale that defies imagination. It takes us half an hour to find the chapel, even though it is tantalisingly signed all over the place. We wander around in circles, up stairs, down stairs, through doors, into courtyards, back up stairs again to find ourselves in the same spot we have just left. But what a walk. One section we pass is crammed with marble statues of animals, each being violently attacked by others. It is all gruesomely fascinating. Before we finally stumble into the ceiling room, a recorded voice from a speaker tells us over and over to be quiet, do not speak, absorb it all for a few minutes and to move on quickly to let other tourists in. Rule-abiding people that we are, we stop talking (we haven't been saying much to each other anyway, thirty-plus years of marriage tends to do that), but when we enter this grand and sacred place we see several hundred people standing around nattering noisily as though at a free-booze cocktail party. We are shocked by such disrespect, but even more so by the ceiling; its repainted colours are too bright, too new and too fake. We stand with our necks craned back as far as they will go and after a while the full awesome measure of it hits us. The paintings are so perfectly scaled and so astonishingly detailed it is impossible to believe that one man lay on his back for sixteen years to paint this. We stare and stare until our heads feel as though they've been permanently affixed to our backs and we then move out like well-behaved tourists, and not just because we really do need a pizza.

Outside in the heat again, with aching necks, we search for a small café and find one that is packed, jovial and inviting. We stagger in, secure the only table left and have our pizza and a jug of house wine delivered to the table within minutes. We are delighting in being in a lively café full of locals enjoying simple food, but then a large woman gets up and ties a pair of underpants to the end of a stick, holds it up high and every person in the restaurant rises as one large body and follows. A tour group. (She didn't really put underpants on the stick, it was a scarf, but I thought I'd colour the story up a bit.) We are annoyed to think we have been surrounded by a group of tourists in what we thought was a locals' place. We are cheered slightly, however, when a woman dashes out of the toilets to alert the departing group that two of the old ladies have been locked in the lavatory. The group files back in and has to wait another fifteen minutes until someone calls for a locksmith to let the old ladies out. See what happens when you get old and go on group tours?

Later, the waiter refuses to accept our credit card—cash only—and, seeing our annoyance, offers us a complimentary glass of Limoncello. He brings a bottle to the table and, stupidly, leaves it there.

We head tipsily back to our hotel room for a much-needed siesta and, after tripping over each other in the few centimetres of space around the bed, flop down and turn on the television. We search and fail to find CNN, so we settle for what looks like an Italian current affairs program and watch inanely, not understanding a word.

While travelling I thoroughly enjoy watching local television and getting caught up in the news, both good and bad. This is especially so when I am touring Australia. The further you go into country areas, the more fascinating the local news becomes, but it is perhaps not quite so absorbing as the commercials that interrupt it. I have learnt many a useful thing from regional television commercials, especially the ones made by the business owners themselves, and even more especially the ones made by farmers. I could now quite confidently put my arm up a cow's bum to administer a spot of nursing should I ever be required to do so, and I know how to control tapeworm and ticks in sheep. My favourite homemade commercials are the ones made by the overweight matronly owner of the local fashion boutique—usually a place named Beth's Oasis of Fashion or Gladys's Island of style— that sells the style of garments your grandmother put out in the ragbag twenty years ago. This woman enlists the help of other overweight matronly women to model the latest summer fashions now in stock. The models sit stiffly at a country kitchen table in their new crimplene slacks and floral linen jackets sipping coffee and eating cake while the owner does an atrociously daggy voice-over. I love it.

Sometimes I fret over small items of local news because they are important at the time and I'm powerless to do anything about them. In a small place in northern Tasmania, I learnt that employees at the local paper mill were all to be made redundant because of a worldwide oversupply of copy paper. There was no need for them to come to work tomorrow or ever after because the planet was so oversupplied with copy paper there would probably never be a need to manufacture another sheet of it ever again. I bet you've never even given thought to the purchasing of copy paper, have you? But there in northern Tassie, a whole lot of people's lives depended on us buying this most ordinary of products. I remember finding this particularly upsetting at the time, because the area wasn't exactly a hive of industry, although it was a rugged and beautiful part of Tasmania. I worried about the people living there, those who had mortgages and kids to educate and feed and had now lost their jobs at the paper mill. The quiet town didn't look like it had much to offer in the way of alternate employment for anyone, even part-time jobs for the school kids. This vexed me deeply during my two-day stopover and I vowed to buy a warehouse-load of copy paper when I got home. Of course I didn't, because within an hour of leaving the area I had forgotten the place existed. Well, you would have too.

Rome's underground train system is marvellously efficient and cheap. For the equivalent of $1.50, we can ride all over the city and escape the terrible summer heat for a short while. Our favourite part is when we get out at our stop. We come up from beneath the ground, where we have just shot through dark tunnels in a sleek capsule, to find ourselves standing right in front of a fabulous monument. The Colosseum stop is breathtaking; coming up the steps from the underground to gaze on one of the world's most famous monuments is an extraordinarily uplifting experience.

The ancient structure is over 160 feet high and in its glory days could accommodate fifty thousand spectators. We attach ourselves to as many English-speaking groups as we can get away with to listen to the gory history as tour leaders describe the action that went on in ancient times. Gladiators used to enter the Colosseum via one of eighty doors, but only a part of the full structure survives—and not because it collapsed, but because later Italians used the building as a quarry, stealing the stones to build St Peter's and many palaces. And you thought that big chunk was missing because of age and earthquakes, didn't you? And if I hadn't snuck up on that tour group, I wouldn't have been able to pass that bit of fascinating history on to you. Nor would I be able to tell you that it wasn't just gladiators and lions that fought in the Colosseum, it was all sorts of animals including dogs and wild ostriches and donkeys, all captured and brought to the Colosseum and kept below ground along with the prisoners in pens in a maze of corridors. It's impossible to imagine people actually enjoying watching lions tear poor souls to death, isn't it? Or to envisage spectators out for a bit of happy Saturday evening theatre sitting in a Colosseum floodlit by human torches—prisoners bandaged from head to toe in rags soaked in some flammable liquid, tied up high on poles and set alight? Apparently they burned for hours and gave off good light. It makes you tremble with fear and revulsion, doesn't it?

I am awe-struck by the structure, the ruins, the atmosphere. I use two rolls of film and take seventy-two photos of Geoffrey in a green hat and backpack posing against various bits of the Colosseum. And an impressive backdrop it is, too, but one photo would have sufficed, as our (now ex-) friends will vouch for after sitting through an endless evening of pretending to enjoy our holiday album.

Workmen are erecting a flat platform in the centre of the Colosseum, on top of the ruins. It is for an upcoming concert and I can't imagine anything more culturally thrilling that to be in this space watching a concert on a hot summer's night, particularly when there is little chance of witnessing a lion rip someone's head off, and electricity provides all the lighting needed. We later learn that a concert has indeed taken place, the first time the Colosseum has been used to entertain since ancient times.

The only positive thing that can be said about our hotel room is that the small window overlooks the large bathroom in a hotel across the street where a well-built man spends a lot of time standing naked in front of the mirror. As a result, I spend a lot of time with my head stuck to the window, which is just as well because otherwise I would go stark raving mad in the small room.

We spend our last day in Rome wandering the hot streets and feeling guilty that we are not admiring more sculptures, statues and paintings, but are instead looking for a fake handbag.

Over the past couple of days I have seen a few shifty-eyed African men selling rip-off Louis Vuittons on blankets on the footpath and have approached them with generous offers one one-hundredth of their asking price. They have refused to bargain and I have walked away haughtily, thinking there would always be another chance for a better deal another day. But there is no time left now. It has to be today or not at all, so of course there is no sign of a handbag or a shifty-eyed African man anywhere. We walk for hours in the heat, wilting, searching, until we finally find the desired blanket spread out on the footpath with a dozen Louis Vuittons of all shapes and sizes on display. I don't care what I have to pay now, I just want one. I also want to get back to our cool hotel room and our shower and my naked man across the road.

But just as I am about to negotiate, police sirens sound and a second African man appears from around the corner, waving his arms and frantically shouting warnings. The bags are wrapped up in the blanket in seconds, just before the police car screeches onto the footpath. The man and his bags race off into the crowded streets with the police pursuing him on foot. They catch him and drag him back, shoving him and his bags into the car while everyone stares amusedly except me, who stares despondently. You should learn a small lesson from me: always buy that special thing you want—especially if it is a rip-off special thing—when you first have the chance. I went home Louis Vuitton-less and have remained so ever since.

We return to our horrible hotel, where I have another look at my naked man across the street and then we pack. Rome and its myriad treasures that we did not get around to seeing will have to wait for another year. For now we are going back to Tuscany for a short while.

Eighteen

Our arrival in Siena is not a dignified one. As on other Tuscan forays, we are lulled into foolish complacency by the charm of the countryside and drive confidently into the outskirts of Siena a little dazed by the beauty. Before we realise it, we are speeding blithely through the opening in the ancient wall surrounding the city, right into the labyrinth of narrow streets inside.

There is no going back on this one-way street, so we carry on, expecting to suddenly pop out the other side. With each turn, however, the roads become narrower and more constricted until we are in a tightly paved laneway so clogged with tourists that we are forced to a complete standstill.

People flatten themselves against walls and shop windows and are stuck against our car; they stare angrily at us through the windows, some giving us the kind of looks usually reserved for messy drunks at weddings the moment before they throw up on the bride's dress.

We are embarrassed more than anything else. Our typical care-less attitude when preparing for this small journey from Rome to Siena means that we have not studied maps carefully nor consulted our guidebooks to see if car access is actually permitted inside Siena's walls.

People try to unglue themselves from the car and squeeze around us while Geoffrey and I sit there, red and sweaty, uttering foul words at each other.

'Why did you bring us in here? It's obviously not for cars!' I hiss, as more and more people come out from lovely shops to find them-selves stuck in the crush.

'You do better, you didn't help, you could have read the map', he replies. You know the sort of argument I'm on about: blame, blame, blame.

It is the driver of a small delivery truck who finally saves us. He inches his truck through the crowd, right up behind us until we are almost touching, then puts his hand on the horn and presses. And doesn't stop. The noise is unrelenting and finally the crowd slowly peels itself off our car and melts into shop doorways, leaving us a small space to move.

We are forced to drive at pedestrian pace to allow the sea of people to slowly part around us. For the next hour we continue snail-like through throngs of people, down endless narrow streets in search of a hole in the wall. Often we find ourselves back on the same street we had been stuck on fifteen minutes earlier, bogged in by flesh all over again. I don't think we have ever known such aggravation. It is quite possible that we could be lost inside Siena until the end of the tourist season, maybe even the end of time. There seems to be no hope of ever getting back outside these lovely walls to wide, people-free roads. It is late afternoon and every person in Tuscany seems to have descended upon Siena for their *passeggiata*. We long for the comfort of our hotel and a desperate delve into our gin bottle. Finally we turn off the engine, slither out of the car, leave it mid-street surrounded by glaring people and race into a café to beg for directions.

'*La macchina? La macchina?*' the shopkeeper asks in both amazement and alarm. The car? The car? You actually brought the car in here?

'Yes, stupidly, accidentally, not on purpose, of course. Please help us get out of here', we plead. He speaks rapidly to a group of old men hunched over a card game at a nearby table. They fall into gleeful laughter and look out the window to our abandoned car, now almost invisible beneath swarms of irritated people.

We wave our map at the men, pointing to our hotel, so close yet so very far away. They examine the map thoughtfully and break into that kind of argumentative conversation Italians use whether they're excited or not, until finally one of them comes out to the car with us. He shouts at the crowds, as old Italian men are allowed to do, and they slowly peel themselves off the car and press back against the walls. He points carefully with his finger to a line on the map that leads to our hotel and, after a further fifteen confusing minutes, at which point we are almost delirious with frustration, we suddenly shoot back out through an opening in the wall into a proper wide street with speeding cars and not a single person on the road. We burst into tears.

We find our hotel straight away, across the road from the wall. In our room at the back of the hotel, which overlooks green Tuscan hills and ancient buildings, we rummage through our suitcases for the bottle of gin. Geoffrey goes immediately to the small bar downstairs to buy tonic water from a suspicious bar person who is mystified as to why anyone would want to drink in their hotel room when there are lively bars aplenty on every corner. But we are desperate.

As we drink we look in our guidebook, turn to the pages on Siena and read. 'In Lucca, Siena and San Gimignano, only residents and taxis may drive inside the city walls.'

Once settled and fortified, showered and dressed, relaxed and apologetic for the filthy accusations exchanged in the car, we set off on foot to explore.

A *cartina della città* (map of the city), shows a pedestrian opening in the wall. This leads to a flight of ugly escalators, an awful, modern surprise among the ancient beauty. Within a few minutes we are inside Siena proper once again, this time as confident as the other tourists, ready for walking, ready for anything, so long as the wretched car is safely out of sight.

Our guidebook tells us that Siena reached its peak of splendour in the early fourteenth century, when most of the monuments were built, but the town was then 'laid low' by the Black Death in 1348. An amusing understatement: it wiped out almost everyone in Siena and the town faded to obscurity for a long time. There is nothing obscure about it now, though; it definitely holds promise of the 'jewel of world wide fame', as our guidebook tells us.

It is about eight in the evening, a lovely cooler time when the streets are not so clogged. We clack along the cobblestones, holding hands, passing lovely shops full of expensive handbags and shoes, beautiful homewares and huge rustic platters that would look sensational full of lemons back at home on my dining table. We love Siena immediately.

No guidebook, no amount of vast research, nothing, could have prepared us for the jaw-dropping beauty of the Piazza del Campo. As we enter it from the bottom of the steps, we stop, rigid with disbelief that we humans could have created anything so beautiful. I feel sure everyone who enters this *piazza* for the first time has this reaction; indeed, anyone entering it for the hundredth time would surely feel the need to stop for a few moments to stare in awe and admiration.

The remarkable buildings around the *piazza* represent everything that is evocative and inspiring about another age. Built in the thirteenth and fourteenth centuries, thanks to plenty of money donated by wealthy citizens, this centre of town is unique (as far as *piazza*s go) for its shell shape and brick floor divided into nine clearly marked sections. Its focal point for me is the soaring *Torre del Mangia* (Mangia Tower), a red-brick building that climbs imperiously high up into the brilliant blue sky. The guidebooks will tell you that the focus of the *piazza* is the *Fonte Gaia* (Gay Fountain), a wide square marble basin decorated with statues, but I could not tear my eyes from the Torre del Mangia. The fountain is lovely, though, a modern copy of the original, which was removed to prevent it deteriorating from the weather.

We stand and stare around the *piazza* for a long time, trying to imagine what it was like during the construction, the place swarming with architects, workers, slaves and young artists commissioned to paint the frescoes. Siena is home to some of the most valuable art in Tuscany, yet at this time of evening, all anybody seems interested in is partying. All around the *piazza*, cafés, bars and restaurants have put out chairs and tables and the place is packed with people eating and drinking. It is just a matter of days before *Il Palio*, the famous bareback horserace around the *piazza*, and there is an atmosphere of expectation and festivity.

We find a table among the throng and sit and stare at the surroundings. Pizzas are the only fare on offer at this café, but this is fine because we could be fed anything and still be happy. As we munch our way through a small, overpriced tomato-and-cheese pizza and launch into a carafe of good, inexpensive wine, we watch the people at *passeggiata*. The constant stream circling the *piazza* is enough to make us dizzy. Around, around and around again they go, gorgeous young things in cropped tops and jeans, young parents pushing prams and carrying toddlers, middle-aged couples sauntering, old grandparents shuffling. It is a wonderful procession of people enjoying themselves on a warm summer night through a simple ritual of walking, and their pleasure gives us pleasure. As we sit and watch our way through several pizzas and far too many carafes of wine, we are as wholly content now as we were terribly frustrated earlier.

We are then treated to a sight unlike any we have seen before, as young men and boys appear, dressed from head to foot in brilliant mediaeval-style costumes, some in yellow, green, purple and blue outfits of tights and small tunics that just skim their bottoms, others in imposing gold-trimmed red robes and tall hats. They carry large bright flags on long poles and elaborately decorated drums in colours to match their outfits. Fifteen or twenty of them line up in groups and, with grand thumps on their drums, march around the *piazza* with mediaeval-style pageantry. They then stop right in front of us and treat us to a display of impressive flag-throwing accompanied by excited shouts and yelps. This exhibition is obviously part of the pre-Palio activities. *Il Palio* is one of Italy's most celebrated and famous festivals and we are thrilled to have chosen this time to visit. Il Palio dates back to the early thirteenth century and is now one of the hottest tickets in town. Celebrities and rich people pay huge sums for spots on the balconies overlooking the *piazza*, and I well remember television scenes of Fergie standing royally on one of the balconies smiling and waving at the hoi polloi crammed into the middle of the *piazza*. Like our Melbourne Cup, there is much anticipation and money exchanged before the event, but the actual race of Il Palio lasts only ninety seconds. I don't know whether it stops the nation like the Melbourne Cup does, but the preparations all around us indicate that this may be so.

We stay until the sun has long gone, the people have stopped walking and the *piazza* is lit up for the night, taking on even more magnificence. We leave reluctantly around eleven o'clock, vowing to return first thing in the morning to soak up the atmosphere again.

Unfortunately, it isn't so atmospheric in the blazing heat of the early morning without the people at *passeggiata* or the cafés buzzing with revellers, so we leave and wander through the backstreets. We have coffees and square slabs of pizza at a noisy café and then visit the *duomo* (cathedral) in Piazza del Duomo, which is one of the most spectacular in Italy. It was built in full Gothic style and is yet another icon that can easily take your breath away on entry, especially if you are prone to vertigo and gaze upwards to the towering ceiling—its height and grandeur creates a need to reach out to clutch something or someone for balance.

The cathedral holds too much splendour to take in during one visit, too many exquisite frescoes covering the walls and inlaid marble floors, too many artworks and famous names—Michelangelo, Bernini, Donatello, Pinturicchio. It was the ordinary people who carted the massive black-and-white stones used in its construction from quarries on the outskirts of the city. The plan was to build the biggest church in Christendom and in 1339 a new nave to the south was started, but the plague hit and halted things for a while—as plagues do—and the nave remains unfinished. Even so, this is one of the biggest and most exquisite cathedrals in Italy.

Places of such grandeur always make me feel at first awed, then humbled, then stupid. After the impact has hit me between the eyes and I have adjusted to the humble feeling of being in such a hallowed and sacred place, I start to wonder how a building of such enormity has been achieved. I know it took a few hundred years to complete, but the manpower involved must have been mind-boggling; thousands upon thousands of people must have worked on this place over the years. I cannot help but stare and stare at the enormous marble columns; I touch their smooth surface, trying to connect with the poor souls who probably died trying to erect them. I stare up to the ceiling until I'm giddy and strained from trying to think how anyone could have achieved such artwork while lying flat on scaffolding in such an awkward position. It all becomes overwhelming and that's when I feel stupid. I simply can't take it all in.

Although there are many visitors in the cathedral on this hot July day, its vastness makes it appear almost empty. It is cool and so very serene in here and we stay a long time, so long that we are mar-velled-out. Then, all of a sudden, there is a further thrill. A group of children and young people come to the altar for choir practise. Their sweet voices soar up to the airy heights of the monumental ceiling and goose bumps break out over our arms. We are having too many lucky happenings in Siena and do indeed feel blessed. Our time in Siena is too brief. We need more time here to get to know the city, to further explore its intriguing backstreets and to sit and sit and sit in the marvellous *piazza* all over again.

Another year we will go back, maybe wrangle a ticket to Il Palio, perhaps rub shoulders with some of Europe's high society on the balcony. There I go fantasising again; I'd be lucky to score a ticket down there in the middle with the masses.

Next we travel to Lucca, which, for some inexplicable reason, just doesn't do anything for us. Perhaps Siena's astonishing beauty overwhelms everything else, perhaps we have no more gasps of astonishment left in us, perhaps our eyes have rested on too much stateliness and splendour these past weeks. Lucca must be visited another year, when we first arrive in Italy, without the detour to Siena. We need to be able to give Lucca the respect it deserves.

Our hotel in Lucca doesn't do anything to put us in the mood for history and atmosphere. It is one of those chain-group hotels and is about ten minutes outside the town, outside the walls. We could be anywhere in Australia in such a charmless hotel, but it is clean and air-conditioned, even if it lacks the historical appeal of some of its counterparts in other Italian cities. We have dinner in the hotel dining room because we can't be bothered taking the ten-minute bus ride into town. The dining room is like any other dining room in any other hotel in any other city in the world, except that the waiters wear bow ties and dinner jackets and serve the food with that wonderful sense of importance I've talked about before.

The dining room is full of businessmen eating alone, each dressed in a smart business suit and each with a magazine or book propped before him. We are the only ones not dining alone. The beautifully dressed waiters scurry around, taking ornate silver soup tureens to tables and spooning out watery minestrone at the table as though it is liquid gold. Out they come with trolleys, wheeling big antiquated silver dishes (much like you'd expect to see in the country house of English royalty, if you ever happened to be invited), lifting the impressive silver lids to reveal a colourless blob of plain spaghetti or boring pasta-goo beneath.

In the morning we take the bus into Lucca to give the town another go, to see if we can become inspired all over again. Lucca, like Siena, is enclosed by wondrous and massive brick walls, which give the town its magical, ancient feel. Where traffic is shut out and buildings and laneways are preserved, there is a feeling of stepping back in time, even if the modern signs clinging to ancient walls jar the image. We sit outside at a small café beneath the biggest tree we have ever seen—so large it spreads a canopy over several other cafés—and watch the tourists come and go. Then we wander through the laneways, buy an overpriced sandwich, look unenthusiastically into some of the shops and decide we'd better get out of Lucca, because such a beautiful place deserves a more appreciative audience.

Nineteen

Like so very many people before us, we had dreamt of visiting Tuscany. I remember back in the late seventies and early eighties, when I was immersed in suburbia, telling people that I wanted to holiday in Tuscany, even though I really wasn't sure where Tuscany was. It just seemed to be the very hip (at the time) thing to say.

'Let's holiday in Tuscany next year', I'd say grandly to someone the moment I knew them well enough to want to holiday with them. At that stage I was only vaguely aware that Tuscany was somewhere in Italy where attractive people sat near cypress trees drinking Chianti before taking leisurely strolls and buying tomatoes from old men at roadside stalls.

'Yes, let's do that, we really must', they would mostly reply, not really knowing where Tuscany was either but thinking my idea sounded far too fabulous to reveal their ignorance.

'We could do Umbria as well', someone replied once, and that threw me into a flux because I had no idea where Umbria was, what the locals did there, or whether they also had old men selling red tomatoes by the roadside.

We thought we'd better find out where Tuscany and Umbria were, so we started looking at maps of Italy and its different areas and regions. We soon realised that it would be many years and thousands of dollars later before we could possibly hope for a trip to any of them.

But time really does go by quickly and before we realised it, our three small children had grown into big six-foot-plus things with jobs and minds of their own and had flown from our nest. While this was a sad thing, it also freed up a hell of a lot of money that was previously tied up in paying school fees and buying new, expensive sneakers every week. Before we knew it, it was the mid-nineties and we were making travel plans to go with a group of friends to Tuscany. We got right up to the booking stage—a villa near Radda in Chianti with five bedrooms and sweeping country views and little courtyards and enough bathrooms so we wouldn't have to share—and then had to cancel because we couldn't afford it. This was a great pity, because we had been the organisers. When we backed out, we urged the rest of the group to go ahead without us, but the whole thing fell apart—we like to think this was because the Rickards are such sparkling company that a trip without them would be a dull affair, but in truth, the others couldn't afford it either.

So now, in 2000, driving all over Tuscany and Umbria like real travelling people who not only know where Tuscany is but are pretty damned familiar with Umbria as well, we decide to take a look at Radda in Chianti to see what we missed out on. Chianti also stirs up many memories for us—we were part of the straw-wrapped bottle brigade back in the seventies; we saved dozens of those kitsch bottles and stuck candles in them like just about everyone else in Australia and England and thought they were the height of romantic design at the time.

Chianti wine comes from the Chianti region of Tuscany. Only wines from this region can properly be called Chianti. It is almost impossible for us as Australians with such a short history to comprehend how long things have been going on here in Chianti and how far back wine has been made here. Individual families in Chianti can trace their lines and often land holdings back to the fourteenth and fifteenth centuries. Think about that for a moment. A family that can trace its history back almost a thousand years. How wonderful is that? The first document referring to Chianti wine was apparently written in 1398 by a member of the Fonterutoli family, a family still active in the wine industry today. To think, Geoffrey and I have the Fonterutoli family to thank for those straw-wrapped bottles that brought so much romance to our otherwise dull suburban lives. You may snigger at me and think me a fool, but it is now a joy beyond the telling to sit on a low wall overlooking the green hills surrounding Radda in Chianti and think about the simple pleasure of a straw-wrapped bottle.

We wander through Radda's lovely backstreets, which are full of intriguing wine shops and small, inviting restaurants with tables beautifully set for the evening's festivities. We sit on benches and look out over the views of *Parco Naturale della Viriglia* (the natural park of Viriglia), then wander into the main part of town and look in a glamorous small hotel that has great gorgeousness and stunning country views. We know we would definitely have had a lovely time in Radda with our group of friends, but perhaps it is just as well we didn't go, because most of them are fighting now and don't speak to each other.

Earlier, in June, we had the pleasure of driving unknowingly into one of Italy's most lovely festivals. Luck had us in the small town of Spello, just around the hill from Assisi, and we arrived on the day the town was celebrating its annual dried-flower festival, called *Infiorate*. We only stopped in the town for coffee and a sandwich, and walked through small streets until we came to one that was alive with activity and colour. We had no idea that this was a famous festival where the locals trace chalk outlines on the pavement of the *piazza* and surrounding streets and then scatter dried flowers and fresh petals into the outlines to create floral masterpieces all over the streets. Toothless elderly men worked alongside teenage boys, energetic children helped old widows with worn faces, young women with babies and toddlers bent down with elegant women to sort out sacks of dried flowers and fresh petals of every kind imaginable. Some old ladies sat on wooden chairs by the side of the road and separated the dried flowers into colours while children carefully placed them inside the chalked lines. It was a picture of vivid colour and small-town happiness and we were utterly bewitched. We bought long *panini* filled with bocconcini, tomatoes and basil and sat outside a small café by the road and watched for contented hours as the street slowly became one long, colourful painting.

'This is indescribably wonderful', I said to Geoffrey, who agreed wholeheartedly. We cursed our lack of research yet again because we could have planned an overnight stop in this charming town for this marvellous festival. For a day and a night each June, Spello becomes one great big colouring book. Can you imagine a more beautiful and delightful festival? Later in the afternoon, we walked carefully up and down the streets, admiring the deep reds of the petals and the brilliant yellows and rich golds of the dyed flowers.

We arrive in Pisa in the early afternoon. This place fascinates us, as it does everyone else. The Leaning Tower must be one of the world's most recognisable icons. Geoffrey and I climbed to the top of it in 1970, but I recorded no mention of this in my diary, even though I remember I felt great claustrophobia at the time. I also recall us driving the motorbike right up to the tower and parking it carelessly on a bit of lawn; these days visitors can approach the tower only on foot and must pass a long line of souvenir stalls offering unattractive junk and an unending procession of gypsies out to steal anything not tightly clutched.

I have a photo in which Geoffrey and his motorbike stand next to the tower in 1970, doing that hand thing in the air that everyone does, where you stand well away from the tower and hold your hands up in a propping-up gesture in the hope that you'll look like you're holding up the tower in the photo. No-one does, of course.

This time we approach Pisa with some guidebook foreknowledge. Construction of the Leaning Tower began in 1174—God, these dates make me feel humble—after someone left an architect a few coins in a will and he decided to invest them in marble and build a tower. The tower began to tip sideways before the mediaeval labourers got to the third storey, but they kept going for another seven. Actually, all the buildings in Pisa's Campo dei Miracoli lean—because of sandy soil and shallow foundations—but it is really only the tower that is so famous, because of its spectacular tilt. The tower was finished in 1350 and was, by then, leaning most apparently. It tilted slowly over the next few centuries until engineers and architects from England and France joined in the search for a way to stop the tilt. Things didn't get serious until around 1990, when the Italian government finally closed the tower after a civic tower in Pavia collapsed in 1989 and officials became nervous. There were obviously concerns about the impact the Leaning Tower's closure would have on tourism, so the search for a solution to the tilt became very serious. An urgent exercise in restoration is underway when we visit and the Leaning Tower of Pisa will hopefully stay leaning but secure for many centuries to come.

We see the Leaning Tower from the distance as we approach and it causes us to catch our breath for a moment and emit sighs of 'wow' and 'gosh' and 'golly gee whiz' and other corny stuff, because it really is bloody impressive.

There is, of course, much more in Pisa to make us say 'wow' than just the Leaning Tower. On the lovely manicured green lawns is the beautiful *duomo*. We have a guide take us in and explain some of the many highlights of this Romanesque cathedral, construction of which, he tells us, began in 1063. We sit in the pews as he points out the wondrous frescoes in the dome, the Carrara marble decorating the walls, the carvings, the sculptures and the intricacies of the pulpit's carved supports. We sit enthralled during his narration, and when he finishes we leave this sanctified and holy place and make our way back out through the gaggle of thieving gypsies and junk-selling stallholders.

Next we go to San Gimignano, mainly because we have recently watched *Tea with Mussolini* on video and know this is one hell of a charming place. The approach is part of the thrill, with the tall towers piercing the sky and setting the scene for a romantic visit. The car park outside the city walls quickly erases any hope of romance, with a surly attendant and queue of cars filled with angry drivers fighting for the last empty space. Hours later, after parking kilometres away and walking back, we finally enter San Gimignano and feel that, apart from the throng of tourists flooding the streets in unwashed T-shirts and shabby shoes and carrying huge backpacks, we could be right back in the twelfth century, when construction of the towers began. I find it a constant source of amazement that any government can maintain such beautiful and ancient places so close to their original form. San Gimignano really is the 'city of beautiful towers', and fourteen of the original seventy-six still stand. Their rich owners built the windowless towers as private fortresses and big show-off buildings. We walk through the lovely but crowded streets along with the thousands of other tourists and blend in because, if the truth be told, we wear unwashed T-shirts and shabby shoes ourselves, and I'm sorry for being a snob just back then. We stop for good coffee and delicious cake in one of the many cafés lining the streets, resist buying tea towels with pictures of the towers on them from souvenir shops and finally walk into the Piazza della Cisterna, surrounded by ancient *palazzi*. We sit on the steps and watch the action for a long while, then wander into a church, but a little man wants us to pay money to enter and we refuse. Then we wander off around corners and hear music played by angels. We follow, enchanted, and find an old man playing a harp while a crowd looks on and throws money into his upturned hat. The haunting music floating all around us seems appropriate in this magical setting. Buskers all over the world should play such beautiful music; there should be a law.

We leave San Gimignano reluctantly, for it is now time to return to Rome for our flight back to Australia. You may think we have wandered aimlessly all over Italy, starting in Switzerland, going down to Piemonte, then Siena and Lucca, then to Santa Margherita and Portofino and to Capri and Rome and back to Siena and Lucca, and indeed we have. For that is how we wanted to do Italy this summer; we wanted a loose plan and to travel up and down, back and forth and sideways if necessary, because anything is possible in Italy. Although we have covered many hundreds of kilometres, we have only skimmed the surface of charms in this lovely country and maybe that's a good thing. Italy is a place to go back to time and time again, every year if we can. And we intend to.

Twenty

Saying goodbye to Italy fills us with sadness. For a few months we have forgotten all the everyday small cares back home in Australia. For these fleeting weeks it has been almost impossible to even think of Australia. We simply have not had any news of it. Every day we have scoured the international newspapers looking for something, anything that might have been happening at home, but apart from a tiny paragraph one day about a dreadful fire in a backpacker hostel in Childers in Queensland, there hasn't been a word. One lousy paragraph for so much tragedy and heartbreak. But then, we have to remember that international mega-disasters in far flung places where a few thousand people die in a horrific accident or one of nature's temper tantrums don't register much with Australians.

Our flight, we have been told, is over-booked by more than two hundred people. We find this difficult to believe, because two hundred people is almost another entire planeload, but for some unexplained reason our seats are not confirmed, and as a result we head to the airport six hours ahead of our flight in order to be first in line when the check-in counter opens. We feel inclined to blame the Italians' endearing but frustrating lack of organisation when it comes to bookings, and we wish we'd taken the trouble to go back to Heathrow to fly out in an orderly British fashion.

After a stupendously boring four hours—made worse because all I have to read is a Sidney Sheldon novel—the check-in counter finally opens and we are indeed first in the line. We approach the pleasant young man with our usual polite, *'Parla Inglese?'*, which of course he does, so we then launch into our prepared pleading speech, starting with an old sick mother waiting for us to return so she can let go and die and finishing with an offer to empty the vomit bags on board if only he will let us on this flight. Confused (I wonder why?), he calls for his supervisor while the queue behind us grows longer and tetchier.

Out comes a drop-dead handsome Italian man (thick head of dark hair, deep blue eyes, gold braid stripes on his dark blue uniform). He looks at our passports and tickets and, astonishingly, says, 'Ah, Signor and Signora Rickard, I have been expecting you'.

This dazzling man expecting us? Apparently there was some small stuff-up at check-in when we left Australia and the kind person at Brisbane airport, who I have since included in my will, had emailed his counterpart in Rome—this magnificent man standing in front of us—and told him to look out for, and after, us. We are beyond chuffed. To be so recognised is unprecedented PR in our books, so it won't hurt to give the airline a plug. Thai Airways. 'Smooth as Silk' is their motto and this hunk standing before us certainly qualified in that department.

Our astonishment increases with his next sentence: 'I will make room, I will open up the top section of Business Class for you'. I dig my fingernails into my palms to stop myself from launching at him and tongue-kissing him right there and then.

'Here is your invitation into the Business Class lounge. Go and relax, have a drink and wait until you are called', he says. This couldn't possibly get any better. We trundle off in search of the lounge and free drinks, giving a fleeting but sincerely sad thought for the other people who could quite possibly not get on this flight.

Rome's departure lounge sets my blood pulsing. Announcements for flights to London, Paris and Madrid sound so much more glamorous than ours going the other way to Australia. When the announcement comes on for people going to Casablanca to please board, I have to force myself to sit still, to stop rushing up and begging to be taken with them.

How thrilling does Casablanca sound? And just who does go to Casablanca, apart from me (and possibly you) in fantasies? And what do people do in Casablanca, apart from say 'Play it again Sam'?

These destinations must stoke the fires in the imaginations of all travellers. Lovely-sounding places such as Prague, Paris, Barcelona and Santorini must give even the most jaded traveller an injection of enthusiasm. There are more beautiful destinations out there than we could ever hope to see in several lifetimes. I look at the departure destinations on the television monitor and sigh; so much romance on a television screen. Places with names such as Eumundi, Doonan and Cooroy—all spots of green hinterland charm close to where I live—will never cut it for me again.

Someone is watching over us this day. As we are about to board, our Business Class boarding passes gripped firmly in hand, the fabulous man with the gold braid leaps out from nowhere and says,

'Please give me back your boarding passes', then proceeds to rip them up. Horrified, we just stare until he says, 'I have upgraded you to First Class' and hands us two First Class passes. Well, like Bridget Jones did in her diary, I want to shout out, 'Shag me! Shag me!', but of course I don't, because had I done that, we would have been banished immediately from First Class and sent to the back row of Economy.

We are First Class virgins. Never done it before. And it shows. We stretch out our legs and wriggle our feet in the abundant space, fiddle with every knob and button on the seat and, while all the experienced First Classers refuse the champagne and request mineral water, we scoff down three glasses each before the doors have even closed. The lovely Thai flight attendant in traditional Thai dress keeps her beautiful face impassive as we guzzle our way through an entire bottle of French bubbles. Greedy oafs.

'Would you like a complimentary lightweight tracksuit to change into?' she asks.

Would we ever. 'Can we keep them?'

'Of course.'

As the other passengers finish their mineral water, refuse most of the food and turn their seats into beds, we let our buttocks and thighs wander freely inside our comfy tracksuits, and have every bit of trolley action going.

'Iced vodka with your caviar?'

Good heavens, yes. 'Thank you and hurry back with the trolley.' Tiny icy vodka shots slide down our throats and silky black caviar with red onion follows a second later.

Hot and cold hors d'oeuvres are silver-served to us, rare roast beef is carved before us, a bewildering array of colourful vegetables is proffered, and wicked desserts, French and Italian cheeses and a cartload of French wine give us the kind of gastronomic excitation we have not experienced before or ever will again on a plane.

While gentle snoring begins around us, we delve into our little complimentary travel kits and pat exquisite lotions onto our faces and hands and watch movies and down more vodka from the frosty bottle.

Having known this kind of service, just once, allows us to understand why an acquaintance of ours—a man who once always travelled like this but, like many others these days, can no longer afford to—still constantly talks about it. He once said to me while weeping into his handkerchief, 'Never accept a boarding pass in double digits. And never turn right as you enter a plane'. I wish.

This man always tries to sit in seat A, row 1, even if it is on a short domestic flight in Australia. But not for me the first row. I sat up there once on a Brisbane-to-Melbourne flight and while it's nice not having anyone put their seat right back in your lap, it also means you are the first person off the plane and everyone follows you. I once lead an entire planeload of passengers on a ten-minute journey around the tarmac searching for the terminal entrance. Feeling the eyes of a hundred or so frustrated people on my back was not pleasant as I walked around and around, frantically looking for signs to the terminal, pretending I knew where I was going. I led them through vast hangers out towards the fuel depot and it wasn't until we passed signs that read: 'DANGEROUS. ABSOLUTELY NO ADMITTANCE. ENTRANCE STRICTLY FORBIDDEN. PISS OFF OUT OF HERE' that they realised I had no idea where I was going and they broke off into small huffy groups.

A similar thing happened to me in a small tin shed masquerading as an airport lounge in the Isle of Pines in New Caledonia. As fifty of us waited in the drafty shed to board our plane, I decided to walk briskly to the door to see what was happening outside. Within seconds a queue of forty-nine excited people bearing large pieces of hand luggage lined up behind me; they were not about to back off either, because they thought the plane was boarding. I stood there with them all pressed urgently behind me for twenty awful minutes until the boarding call finally came and mercifully ended my embarrassment.

But, back to the trip home from Italy. Coming back to Australia is quite a shock for us, probably because we tried to hold onto the feeling of being elegant Italians. It hits us before we even disembark from the plane. In some strange way it is awful, yet comforting. The video shown just before landing must frighten the hell out of first-time visitors. A smiling Australian man, usually in a pair of very short navy shorts and long beige socks, tells them he will put them in jail and leave them to rot if they so much as dare to have an apple in their handbags. And don't even dream of bringing in a sausage, otherwise it's off to some dark place for a spot of bamboo-under-the-finger-nail torture before deportation for them.

If the video amuses me and convinces me I am well and truly back in Australia, then the staff at the duty free shops just before immigration control emphasise it.

'Any ciggies with that?' the girl asks in a twangy Aussie accent as I stock up on Baileys and Kahlua. And when she calls out to a fellow staff member, 'Tommo, tell Nevo to get Johnno to bring out more Kahlua', I know I have well and truly arrived home. I love it.

In immigration, as those cute but lively dogs leap on me and sniff my handbag, I am convinced (as always) that someone has surreptitiously slipped a salami onto my person. I become rigid with guilt, convinced every security camera in the immigration hall is focused on my face. I try to relax my features into a picture of carefree innocence, but I know that sneaky, sly and shifty fight for top position over my countenance.

But my most favourite thing about coming back to Brisbane Airport is the presence of two Indian men, complete with splendid blue turbans and moustaches and beards. They usually sit side by side in the booths at passport control, inspecting and stamping passports and passing people through to the baggage collection area.

These exotic men, so visually foreign yet employed to gatekeep at one of our international airports, signify everything that is accepting and multicultural about our society. Apart from a few disgraceful redneck racists whose ignorance never fails to astound me, Australians really are a broadminded and open bunch of people. And seeing these two turbaned Indian men at passport control epitomises everything that is culturally exciting about our country.

Our first day back in Australia keeps getting better and better. I dump my suitcases at home and rush out to do some shopping and stop off at the bakery for some bread.

'Our finger buns are on special today', the woman at the bakery tells me and I could kiss her. Where else in the world could you buy something so vulgarly named? And with such garish pink icing that tastes so comforting?

At my next stop, the post office, the man behind the counter concludes my transaction with an 'okey dokey' and my heart soars. There is much to love about this country and it isn't until we've been away that we remember this.

We really do still call Australia home, but have already begun planning our next trip. Our experience in Italy has inspired us to go again and again. The Italian-language lessons will continue until I can confidently get on the right trains and buses and book hotel rooms and have the courage to stand up for myself in front of aloof signoras. Although I did not receive one single call of *bella donna* nor an offer to 'dance' with a dashing man in uniform, I have still been as thrilled with Italy as I was that first day I stepped off the ship in Naples in 1966 (and I blame Geoffrey's presence for the lack of *bella donnas*).

Now, if you don't mind, it is time to leave you. I am in need of a cuppa and a finger bun. Although ... upon flicking back through the pages of this book, I think a telephone call to ascertain the time and whereabouts of my nearest AA meeting might be more appropriate.

About the Author

Ann Rickard is a London-born, Melbourne-raised, Noosa-based feature writer. After spending ten years working and living in the United Kingdom, Ann and her New Zealander-cum-Australian husband, Geoffrey, settled in Australia, where Ann spent the next twenty years writing, raising her family and dreaming of revisiting Europe. Her feature stories and weekly column in the *Sunshine Coast Daily* have endeared her to readers, and although she is a self-confessed 'old sheila' and writes thousands of words for her newspaper each week, this is her first book.

Go to www.annrickard.com to see Ann's slideshow of Italy.

First published in Australia in 2004 by
New Holland Publishers (Australia) Pty Ltd
Sydney • Auckland • London • Cape Town

14 Aquatic Drive Frenchs Forest NSW 2086 Australia
218 Lake Road Northcote Auckland New Zealand
86 Edgware Road London W2 2EA United Kingdom
80 McKenzie Street Cape Town 8001 South Africa

National Library of Australia Cataloguing-in-Publication Data:

Rickard, Ann (Ann J.).
Not another book about Italy.

ISBN 1 74110 059 3.

1. Italy—Anecdotes. 2. Italy—Humor. 3. Italy—Description and travel.
I. Title.

914.5

Publishing Manager: Robynne Millward
Project Editor: Claire de Medici
Designer: Karlman Roper
Production Manager: Linda Bottari
Printer: McPherson's Printing Group, Victoria

10 9 8 7 6 5 4 3 2 1